IT'S A GOOD THING

Children

are a

Treasure

...They've Broken All
My Other Ones

Group

Loveland, Colorado

Group resources actually work!

This Group resource incorporates our R.E.A.L. approach to ministry. It reinforces a growing friendship with Jesus, encourages long-term learning, and results in life transformation, because it's

Relational
Learner-to-learner interaction enhances learning and builds Christian friendships.

Experiential
What learners experience through discussion and action sticks with them up to 9 times longer than what they simply hear or read.

Applicable
The aim of Christian education is to equip learners to be both hearers and doers of God's Word.

Learner-based
Learners understand and retain more when the learning process takes into consideration how they learn best.

IT'S A GOOD THING CHILDREN ARE A TREASURE...
They've Broken All My Other Ones
52 Devotions for Moms Who Need a Moment With God

Visit our websites: **group.com** and **group.com/women**

This book was written by moms for moms. Each author's name is included with the devotion she wrote. An extra special thanks to Jody Brolsma, Sherri Smith, Brenna Strait, and Melissa Towers, who added ideas for moms to do with their kids.

Unless otherwise indicated, all Scripture quotations are taken from the *Holy Bible*, New Living Translation, copyright © 1996, 2004, 2007, 2013. Used by permission of Tyndale House Publishers, Inc., Carol Stream, Illinois 60188. All rights reserved.

ISBN 978-1-4707-1348-5

10 9 8 7 6 5 4 3 2   23 22 21 20 19 18 17 16 15

Printed in the United States of America

Contents

Contents cont.

Introduction:

God Loves Moms!

I was in the kitchen and heard a thundering of feet pounding up the stairs.

"Mom! Dad broke the coffee table!"

Yes, my son was telling on his dad!

It turns out that father and son were doing their best Elvis Presley impressions, and my husband had jumped onto the coffee table as a makeshift stage… cracking it right down the middle. This delighted my son, since he was the one who most often broke stuff when roughhousing with dad. Lamps, windows, couch cushions—I'd learned quickly that having a boy in the house meant putting my treasured breakables into storage.

So I laughed at their mishap, and helped carry the split table to the pile for the dump.

Psalm 127:3 says, "Children are a gift from the Lord." Other translations use the word heritage or inheritance. A popular song uses the word treasure. And that's what this book is about. Reminding us that no matter how stressful and frustrating and intense life is for moms, our children truly are gifts from God.

Each devotion was written to encourage you on your journey through momhood. And along the way you'll find a few ideas to help you connect with other moms (every journey is better when you're with a friend or two) and fun ideas for things you can do with your children.

My own son who once told on his dad is now grown and a parent himself. Now I get to be a grandmom—and also celebrate the joys of seeing my son as a young father who loves God—and his daughter. I hope you find joy in motherhood—and encouragement to find that joy on the pages of this book!

Amy Nappa

—Amy Nappa and the Women's Team at Group

It's a Good Thing Children Are a Treasure…They've Broken All My Other Ones

> **"Three things will last forever—faith, hope, and love—and the greatest of these is love."**
> —1 Corinthians 13:13

No one challenges our Christ-likeness the way our children do. When my teenager had disciplinary issues in middle school and ran away from me on the school campus, I knew I was not acting with the love of Jesus as I searched for him. Every time my middle child threw a temper tantrum in the grocery store, the first words that sprang to my lips were not gentle. And when my youngest spilled all kinds of family "secrets" to her Bible study teacher, I ached to become invisible—but not before sealing her lips.

While it's true my kids challenge my Christ-likeness with their antics, they also encourage me with their expectations of Jesus, and the way they show his character.

We were experiencing a typical chaotic morning with phone calls, home school duties, dinner preparation, and errands. Add in the frequent requests for bathroom assistance, boo-boo kissing, a blanket fort in the living room, a story, a dance, a dog walk, and my head was spinning. Remembering my father, who counts to 10 in an attempt to stay calm, I began to recite 1 Corinthians 13.

"Love is patient and kind."

Yet another shout from the bathroom blew my efforts at patience and kindness.

However, when I emerged from the bathroom, I found one of my middle child's tokens of love. Five years old, he delights in drawing pictures and writing "Mommy" or "Daddy" on the outside and then depositing the folded paper in a place we'll see it.

This busy morning, I saw his note taped to the wall and smiled at the blue ink-filled heart. But what he taped above the paper made me laugh out loud and forget my frustration. My son attached one of his younger sister's dirty socks to the wall.

His love note reminded me of his tender heart, and of Jesus' desire to speak into my children's lives through me, their mother. The brief break in frantic activity encouraged me to respond with the same tenderness of heart—even in the middle of daily chaos. And then to do a load of laundry.

| Shelley Ring |

Action Step:

Write a short note to your child today, and share something you love about him or her. If your child doesn't read yet, read the note to him or her. Save it in a memory box or scrap book.

Tweaky DNA

> "So anyone who becomes as humble as this little child is the greatest in the Kingdom of Heaven."
>
> —Matthew 18:4

My youngest child has a tweak in his DNA that puts him outside the spectrum of what we call *healthy*. We make at least four visits a year to Children's Hospital where we are given our marching orders for the next three months. Sometimes these visits remind me that this is not what I imagined as a young pregnant mama. A friend told me that having a baby is like planning a trip. You think you know where you're going...perhaps Ireland...and you pack accordingly, but somehow your plane lands in an equally beautiful place—New Zealand, for instance. But everything you packed is wrong for this trip. That is how I felt when I was adjusting to parenting a chronically ill child. I had not packed for this trip, and I wasn't even sure I wanted to pack for this trip. But here I was...in New Zealand.

I arrived at our next visit to Children's with my 7-year-old in tow. I had my clipboard in hand with our daily schedule. My overflowing notebook with the last five years of medical visits and lab work results was tucked under my arm. My little guy had his bag stuffed with his favorite "buddies" and games for when the day dragged on. I was laser-focused: Don't get in my way; I am a mom on a mission. Before our first appointment, I made a quick pit stop to the ladies room. Then the question, "Mom, do I have to go in there with you? I'm 7..."

"Okay, stay here, I'll be quick."

I step back into the hall where my little one is waiting for me, and that is when I see the real beauty of New Zealand. My fuzzy-headed guy is sitting on the floor with his new bald-headed friend. There isn't really much more to see than their two heads bent close together. I cannot interrupt. I wait. After a little while my sweet treasure looks up at me and simply says, "Okay." He stands up and I take his little hand in mine. "What was that about?" I ask. "Oh, we were just praying for his chemo treatments." And we walked on.

| Dawn Canny |

Action Step:

Intentionally slow down today and get on eye level with a little child. Sit on the floor, walk around on your knees, play a game, sing "Jesus Loves Me" out loud! Ask God to give you a child's perspective, and thank him that you are his child.

Shared Eyeglasses

> **"You made all the delicate, inner parts of my body and knit me together in my mother's womb. Thank you for making me so wonderfully complex! Your workmanship is marvelous—how well I know it."**
>
> —Psalm 139:13-14

"Here we go again! What do I do next, Lord?" These were some of my thoughts when my son was in fifth grade. That year, it seemed I was greeted with problems each day when I picked him up from school. His teacher recited his learning difficulties and the number of times his attention strayed. She detailed specific periods of time he was "off task." I was at my wits' end. I found myself cringing and wanting to avoid contact with his teacher.

My son had a learning disability. There were professionals who believed he also had Attention Deficit Disorder (ADD), and there were those who thought he did not fit the criteria for ADD. A meeting was scheduled at the school with a team of experts. I had such mixed feelings. I was like a mother bear who wanted to protect her cub. At the same time, I was incredibly intimidated at the thought of being surrounded by specialists. I was afraid they only saw my son as a problem to be fixed. My longing was for them to welcome him as a work of art, created by God, a blessing and a person with abilities as well as disabilities.

In my distress, God met me with his Word over and over. He saw my struggle, my fears, and exhaustion mingled with fierce love. It was as if he gave me a pair of eyeglasses I could share with him. Through those lenses I could see my child more clearly. God did not see him as a mistake or just another problem to fix. God created my son. He formed him and made him "wonderfully complex." I would not go into that meeting or any meeting alone. The Lord even provided others along the way to share our eyeglasses. It was an encouragement each time he sent someone to really see my son, to see him as a gift.

Those shared eyeglasses transformed my vision. It was a little easier to leave the defensiveness behind. I could celebrate my son and work with a team of experts to help him grow. Whenever I became confused or afraid, all I needed to do was grab my glasses and cry out to the Lord.

| Rita J. Platt |

Action Step:

Insert your child's name in Psalm 139:13-14 and write those verses down. Keep them somewhere you will see them regularly. Whenever they catch your eye, thank God for your "wonderfully complex" child.

Practice Brings Progress

> "Give your complete attention to these matters. Throw yourself into your tasks so that everyone will see your progress."
>
> —1 Timothy 4:15

"Momma." What a great name. As my children were born, I really didn't realize how wonderful that name (along with "mom") would become. As I sat in the waiting room waiting for the arrival of my first grandchild, I thought about the delivery of both of my daughters. How different it is to see your little girl experiencing childbirth for herself as she eagerly awaits the birth of her first child, a son. How must Mary have felt, as she knew the time of Jesus' birth was near? My daughter delivered in a very comfortable birthing room while Mary delivered in a barn.

Just as childbirth is not easy, being a mom is not always easy either. In fact, it takes a lot of practice and a lot of selflessness on your part. I remember that as a working mom with two small children, I always felt pulled in many different directions. My second daughter was born 26 months after my first, and they were definitely not on the same page in anything they were doing for quite some time. My oldest was always a self-starter and determined to do things her way. One night as I was bathing the baby, I heard a fall and a scream from the other room. As I ran, wet baby in hand, to check on her, I found her on the kitchen counter with a bottle of Benadryl spilled all over the counter. She looked up at me and said, "Look, Momma, I took my medicine." With my husband still at work, I went into a panic and ended up in the emergency room with black, charcoal-type stuff being put into my daughter, since we had no idea how much she had actually taken. Needless to say, that was not one of my better nights.

I needed to practice how to be a mom to two children instead of one. As children grow physically and spiritually, each phase is different and we learn new ways to communicate and grow our relationship with our children. Being a follower of Christ is the same way. We practice and then we see progress. God has given all of us gifts to use for him, and as moms we can help our children discover their gifts by practicing serving God.

Hold your children if they are young, and never quit hugging them. Being a mom is not easy, but it sure is worth the effort. None of us are perfect moms, but if we keep God first and rely on him for directions, we'll see progress from all our practice.

| Eliese McAllister |

Action Step:

Look at your children as they sleep. See how peaceful they look. Thank God for all the peaceful times you have experienced—and also thank him for the chaotic times when you are reminded that he is in control.

It's a Good Thing Children Are a Treasure...They've Broken All My Other Ones

Mom to Mom 1

Get together with one or two moms you know. Take time to talk about which of the devotions you've read recently was most meaningful to you and why. It's okay if you're all at different places in the book—just share what God puts on your heart.

Also, share an area of your life where you could use some prayer. Jot down what others say so you can remember to pray for them this week.

_____

_____

_____

_____

_____

Be sure your time together includes hugs and words of encouragement for each other!

Moms need it!

Mom Time!

Here's something fun to do with your family.

Wacky Ball

Grab a ball and head to a park or driveway that has a basketball hoop. The youngest goes first and tosses the ball in the silliest way possible. If the ball actually goes into the hoop, the next person has to exactly copy that silly throw and try for a basket. If the ball of the youngest player doesn't go in the hoop, the next person gets to make up a new crazy throw. No scoring required—just play for fun and the joy of being together. Want to make it even wackier? Use any ball except a basketball! Football, tennis ball, volleyball—whatever you have!

Pass the Chocolate, Hold the Card

> **"Yes, I am the vine; you are the branches. Those who remain in me, and I in them, will produce much fruit. For apart from me you can do nothing."**
>
> —John 15:5

On my first Mother's Day, I was less sappy and more I-want-to-hide-in-a-hole. It seemed beyond ironic that on a day I had longed for, I felt like a fraud. I feared that I displayed a transparent smile through which everyone could see that I was, in fact, completely undeserving of being celebrated that day.

There were other mothers who dominated the blogosphere and books with perfect parenting advice and deep spiritual truths along with creatively inspired parties, decorations, and recipes; those mothers should be celebrated. But not me. I lost my temper. I wanted more than a few hours of uninterrupted sleep. Oh, how I wanted sleep! I had no clue what I was doing as a parent. At times, I even considered the lie that our infertility was God's way of confirming that I was not fit for motherhood. I was not worthy to be honored. Give me lots of chocolate, but no cards to sing my praises.

I entered parenthood through a 2-year-old child with medical needs whom we had brought home from China less than two months before my first Mother's Day. My whole world had been turned upside down, as was his, and we were all struggling. I needed a lot of grace and strength. And chocolate. And some sleep.

Our years of infertility and the journey of the adoption process had left me a bit ragged, but they transformed me as I learned and experienced God's truth. And one truth was drilled in repeatedly: I can do nothing without God. I am completely dependent upon him for *all* things. Raising a child for the glory of God will be one of the hardest things I ever do. It is a privilege and a sobering realization that I am not the least bit sufficient for the task. But God is. He gives me grace and sufficiency through himself.

We were never expected to do this alone. God is in us to work through us. What I do want my son to remember and love about me is that I cling to the strength of God. I hope I model a relationship with God that reflects utmost dependency, love, and devotion. Those are the things that matter.

| Jenny Riddle |

Action Step:

In a world full of social media in which we intentionally or unintentionally show only the best sides of our lives, it's important to remind ourselves that what's most important isn't always what's picture-worthy. Take a break from social media or your camera phone for a day (or a few hours!). Think of what you want to model for your children and begin to make a plan to practically incorporate those habits into your life.

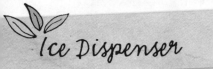
Ice Dispenser

> **"Anyone who believes in me may come and drink! For the Scriptures declare, 'Rivers of living water will flow from his heart.'"**
> —John 7:38

As I sat with a group of young moms, I asked them to describe themselves. One of the ladies quickly responded, "I feel like an ice dispenser." I could so identify with that analogy! As moms, we often feel as though our husbands and children are putting their proverbial buckets under us, always needing something from us. And sometimes we just don't have much to give.

A few weekends later, I was at a jam-packed hotel for a speaking engagement. I went to the vendor area with my bucket to get some ice. I put my bucket under the dispenser and pushed the button. The machine began to make a grinding noise, and after quite some time, one tiny piece of ice fell into my bucket. So many people were at the hotel demanding ice that the icemaker just couldn't keep up. As a mom, I've felt just like that ice dispenser, unable to keep up with all that is needed from me.

When I thought about that weekend at the hotel, I realized something about myself: If I don't continue to let Jesus pour into me, I won't have anything to give.

Instead of my focusing on the fact that everybody wants something from me, what would happen if I focused on making sure I was filled up so that I had something to give when they needed it? Then, instead of begrudging the fact that they always needed me, I could—with delight—offer what they needed because I was already filled and ready to give it.

We often think it selfish to take some time for ourselves, even if it is just a few moments. And yet, if we don't take time to be filled up, we won't have anything to give. The reality is, if we do not replenish ourselves, we end up pouring out selfishness, irritability, resentment, or anger. But if we choose to fill our hearts with the love of Jesus, that's what will pour from us. If we choose to fill our hearts with the peace that Jesus gives, that's what our husbands and children will receive. As my mom used to say, "What's down in the well comes up in the bucket."

| Jena Forehand |

Action Step:

Take a few moments each day to fill your heart with the truths of God. Ask God to fill you with everything necessary to offer others when they come to you in need. Ask God to make you aware of when your "dispenser" is empty, so you can get replenished. Each time you put ice in a glass, ask yourself, "Have I taken time to be filled up today?"

All I Need Is a Noodle

> **"He reached down from heaven and rescued me; he drew me out of deep waters."**
> —Psalm 18:16

I smiled as I looked at the caller ID on my phone. "Hi, Dannielle!" I greeted my sweet friend cheerfully—but I could tell immediately that something was wrong. The news she shared was heartbreaking. She had just been diagnosed with cancer.

Dannielle lived over a thousand miles away. I couldn't take her a meal, go clean her house, or watch a movie with her. Another friend asked if I'd be interested in doing the Susan G. Komen Breast Cancer Foundation Tri for the Cure.

"Me?" I thought, "A *triathlon?*"

I knew this was a way I could show my love and support for Dannielle, but I wasn't really sure I could do it! After all, I swim like a rock! But then my friend let me in on a secret...

On the morning of the tri, standing near the entrance to the water, "angels" in disguise call out, "Anybody need a swim buddy?"

"Yes!" I say, hoping my voice wasn't too loud or desperate. With an encouraging smile and a *swim noodle* firmly in hand, my swim buddy enters the water with me.

"I'm really a terrible swimmer!" I tell her. "Don't worry!" she responds. "Today you're a great swimmer and I'm with you all the way!" She doesn't even care if I'm the slowest gal in the water, doing the *sidestroke* in a triathlon! (Yes, really!) She swims beside me, periodically asks if I'm okay, warns me when someone is close, and guides me while I do the backstroke for a bit.

"Do you want to rest?" She asks kindly. "The noodle is yours whenever you need it!"

Now you know my secret: I did a triathlon for Dannielle thanks entirely to my swim buddy.

Every mom needs a swim buddy from time to time. Someone to speak words of hope and encouragement. Someone to help us navigate murky waters. Someone who'll get right in there with us to cheer us on and give us a break when the going gets tough. Someone who doesn't care if all we can do is the sidestroke. Someone who offers a noodle when we need it!

| DeeAnn Bragaw |

Action Step:

Today, why not send a quick text or make a call to say thank you to someone Jesus has sent to be a swim buddy when you most needed her? And how about looking for another mom who just might need a noodle?

I Think I'm Perfect

"For we are God's masterpiece."

—Ephesians 2:10

"Perfect." That was the name I gave myself at a women's retreat I attended with my daughter during a spiritual exercise we were asked to do. Don't get me wrong. It's not that I think I'm perfect—it's that I realized I still operate out of the belief that I have to be perfect in order to be valued.

So, on to my "perfect" weekend retreat:

- I spilled an entire, large cup of coffee in front of a billion women. (Okay, not a billion, but close.)

- My daughter and I walked past a glass sign for the retreat and lovingly knocked that sucker over, watching it shatter into a million pieces. And I do mean a million.

- I hardly slept the entire weekend and had to lead worship Sunday morning, which of course, I wanted to be "perfect."

- And to top it off, a cute little bird pooped on my bare foot during my quiet time with God. Priceless.

God had a funny way of stripping away all of my perfect self that weekend, leaving me utterly dependent on what I believe he was telling me his name for me was: "Beautiful." Bird poop and all.

I'm not the only one with this problem. Another young lady told me her name was "Crisco," since that was the name her dad called her because she was an overweight child. Another said her name was "Critic." She got that from her mom.

With my daughter by my side that weekend, I was especially aware of how important it is to build into our children their true identities as children of God. Moreover, *I realized that we cannot teach our children who they are until we really own who we are.* The mom who taught that young lady her name was Critic? That was me.

I am so grateful for a God who helped me learn my true identity over the years and whose love broke down my protective walls so that his healing could take place in my life. I'm thankful I can now talk to my children about the harmful names I unknowingly passed down to them, and now share with them their *true* names given to them by their heavenly Father.

| Sherri Stone-Bennett |

Action Step:

Go to your nearest dollar store and pick up a hand-held mirror for each child (and one for yourself). Next, with a list of Scriptures that speak about identity already picked out, have each child read one passage at a time and then write one word that represents that passage with a permanent pen on the front of the mirror, along with the Scripture underneath. For example, for Ephesians 2:10, they might write "masterpiece" with "Ephesians 2:10" below it. Each time they look in this mirror, the words in the background will remind them of their identity in Christ. Here are some Scriptures to get you started: Psalm 139:13-16; 1 Peter 2:9; Ephesians 2:10; Galatians 4:6-7; 1 John 3:1.

Get together with one or two moms you know. Take time to talk about which of the devotions you've read recently was most meaningful to you and why. It's okay if you're all at different places in the book—just share what God puts on your heart.

Also, share an area of your life where you could use some prayer. Jot down what others say so you can remember to pray for them this week.

_____

_____

_____

_____

Consider inviting someone you don't know as well to your mom gathering. An easy way to start is invite her to join you and another mom for coffee or another warm beverage.

Mom Time!

Here's something fun to do with your family.

Walking Scavenger Hunt

You can do this with your young children, or pair up older siblings to play on teams.

On the outside of small paper bags (like lunch bags), write a list of items that can be found in your yard, your house, or nearby in your neighborhood. Then walk and explore together to find the items. So fun and easy! Sample list for outdoor hunt: 1 grey rock, 2 leaves, 3 sticks, 1 small pebble, 1 shiny object, 1 pine cone. Sample list for indoor: 3 building blocks, 2 buttons, 1 pencil, 1 cat (can be real or a toy), 1 ball, 1 item that starts with an S.

Pleasing Aroma

"Live a life filled with love, following the example of Christ. He loved us and offered himself as a sacrifice for us, a pleasing aroma to God."

—Ephesians 5:2

As a mom of a child who has autism, one of the first signs I noticed in my son other than his lack of eye contact was his extreme need for order. He would spend hours lining up his plastic animals trying to get them just so. He would come back five minutes or five hours later and if anything had been even slightly moved, he would absolutely lose it. As with my other children, I would encourage him to take deep breaths to help him calm down. I knew that this was both a distraction and had an actual physiological effect to help his body calm down. However, my son was so literal-minded that taking deep breaths for deep breaths' sake made no sense to him—especially when he was almost out of control. We began buying inexpensive bouquets of fresh flowers. Whenever my son's emotions overwhelmed him, we would snap off a fresh flower and have him breathe in the scent until he began to calm down.

As I read the above verse from Ephesians 5 one day, I was reminded that taking deep breaths and relaxing is something we need to remember to do at every age and stage of our lives. And that it's for more than a physiological response: It's a way to remember Jesus' example of a life filled with love.

I love my son with more passion than I ever thought possible. There are times, though, when I can't connect or communicate with him and I feel frustration and anger. My emotions and actions don't follow the example Christ has set before me. Those are the times I stop and take a deep breath and pray for God's love to fill me completely.

| Amy Weaver |

Action Step:

Take a moment in the midst of your most stressful time today to breathe in a pleasing aroma. Take a whiff of fresh flowers, sniff a scented candle, or step outside for a breath of fresh air. As you do, ask God to fill you with his love. Pray that you'll be an example of Christ and a pleasing aroma to everyone around you, especially your children.

A Master Plan

> "And we know that God causes everything to work together for the good of those who love God and are called according to his purpose for them."
>
> —Romans 8:28

Sometimes as moms, we lose sight of our purpose. Changing diapers, finding lost Legos, helping with homework...the work of bringing up children seems unending and thankless. Remember today that God has a purpose for your life, which goes far beyond an endless stream of runny noses.

Recently, while driving my daughter to school for early choir practice and delivering my teenager to the high school for band rehearsal, I began fretting about everything working out. I was running late for work, and my son still needed breakfast. He looked at me, with a smile on his face. "Don't worry, Mom," he said kindly. "Everything always works out. God has a plan."

From the mouths of babes often comes great wisdom. I took a deep breath and smiled back, feeling much more peaceful.

God does have a plan for your life, and every circumstance you confront today is part of that plan. You don't need to worry or fret, because God's plan for you is a good one. He will hear your prayers, and he will make himself known to you if you are able to pause and listen.

God's plan for our lives includes us raising our children, but it doesn't stop there. Our real task is to teach them love and compassion and forgiveness. Each day presents an opportunity for us to fulfill God's plan and live his message of love for those around us.

Children learn more from our actions than our words. Our actions teach our children who God is in our own lives and who he can be in their lives. You can live your purpose each day, by praying to God and listening for his answer. He will show you exactly where to walk. All you have to do is follow.

| Deborah Demander |

Action Step:

Before you set your schedule today, take a moment to pray. Ask God to show you what he wants for your day. Ask him to make you aware of divine appointments. As you walk through today, remember that every circumstance, every person, and even every problem is a gift from God. He is unfolding his plan for you. Walk with the confidence that you are living God's plan and your divine destiny today and every day.

Merciful Moments

> "Since God chose you to be the holy people he loves, you must clothe yourselves with tenderhearted mercy, kindness, humility, gentleness, and patience. Make allowance for each other's faults, and forgive anyone who offends you. Remember, the Lord forgave you, so you must forgive others."
>
> —Colossians 3:12-13

Life is a journey of lessons. My kids seem to teach me the most poignant lessons, especially when I least expect them.

My oldest son was about 5 and his younger brother was 2. We had been out running errands and shopping for most of the morning. We stopped at a favorite café for a quick lunch before heading back out to finish up our errands. As we sat down and I was getting the boys settled with their lunch, I reached across the table and knocked my drink completely over and into the lap of my 5-year-old. It all happened so quickly, yet my mind saw it in slow motion. My body seemed to stand still, unable to prevent the tragedy from happening. There my precious 5-year-old sat, soaked to the skin with my soda.

Very sweetly, he looked up at me and said, "It's okay, Mommy. I know you didn't mean to do it."

Oh my. What a merciful reaction. I'm pretty sure he hadn't learned that from me! I would hate to think what my reaction would have been had he just dumped his entire drink in my lap. Mercy and forgiveness would not have been the first thought on my mind or words out of my mouth!

All I could do was hug him, clean him up, and thank him for being so kind. He almost seemed bewildered at my emotion. I am so thankful God has given my little boy a heart of mercy, compassion, and forgiveness. His heart didn't know how to react any other way. Now it was my job to nurture that little heart and make sure it never became hardened. As he grew older, I would often catch myself when mercy was in order and I wasn't feeling exactly merciful, remembering his little face and those words…"It's okay, Mommy. I know you didn't mean to do it."

Thankfully, we have a merciful Father in heaven. It is our duty to clothe ourselves in that same mercy and show compassion and kindness to others.

| Jennifer Nystrom |

Action Step:

Once a week, guide your dinner conversation to specific times from the past week when family members were able to practice mercy. Have each person share at least one "Merciful Moment" and how they went about showing mercy.

> **"Mary responded, 'I am the Lord's servant. May everything you have said about me come true.'"**
> —Luke 1:38

The day I brought my oldest son home, I remember being excited. And terrified. He was so small, so precious, and I wanted to be the best mother I could be for him. I read a bunch of books and watched parenting DVDs. I talked to other mothers, and the more I talked, or read, or learned, the more afraid I became. The authors, speakers, and mothers felt so sure of what they told me, but many of them contradicted one another. Everyone had their own theory on the best way to raise children, and I wasn't sure which one I should choose.

I started to question myself. What if I couldn't keep up? How could I be sure I was doing the right things?

Two sons later, I still find myself questioning at times, but I have learned that even when I'm not sure of myself, God is. God chose me to be the mother of my children. What works for others may not always work for us. My family is unique. God put us together because he has plans for my children's lives, and I play an important role in getting them where they need to go. All I have to do is be the person God made me to be. I need to remind myself that I am the Lord's servant, created to be unique. Created to be Dylan and Evan's mom.

For this reason, I have found myself fascinated with the way Mary responded to God when she found out she was going to be a mother. I'm sure she had fears, doubts, and faced a lot more than we do today. But she chose to trust in God, to simply accept God's plan for her life. When I'm doubting myself, I try to think about Mary, about how she overcame so much by just being herself and trusting in God.

| Rebbekka Messenger |

Action Step:

What makes you unique as a mother? What sort of experiences have you had that change your parenting style? Maybe you traveled a lot before having children. Maybe you have a strong relationship with your parents. Whatever it is, God has given you these experiences to use as tools so you can be exactly the type of mother your child needs. Make a list for yourself, write it down, and look at it whenever you're in doubt. Above all, remember that God chose you. You're exactly the right parent for your child.

Get together with one or two moms you know. Take time to talk about which of the devotions you've read recently was most meaningful to you and why. It's okay if you're all at different places in the book—just share what God puts on your heart.

Also, share an area of your life where you could use some prayer. Jot down what others say so you can remember to pray for them this week.

_____

_____

_____

_____

_____

_____

While you're together, ask the other moms to share recent photos they have on their phones or other devices. No mom ever gets tired of sharing pics of her kids or grandkids!

Mom Time!

Here's something fun to do with your family.

Fort Fun

Create a fort using chairs, pillows from couches or beds, and blankets or sheets. If you have a few large boxes, add those to the creation as well. (You'd think this is only popular with younger kids, but a surprising number of teens think this is fun too!) Once your fort is complete, huddle inside to read books or play video games, eat a few snacks, and tell your best jokes.

A Swashbuckler of Peace

> **"I am leaving you with a gift—peace of mind and heart. And the peace I give is a gift the world cannot give. So don't be troubled or afraid."**
>
> —John 14:27

On occasion, I'll be settled in my living room chair, reading or watching TV, when a rush of wind and a blur of color pass at an alarming speed. I can usually identify it as a little boy.

We recently moved to a larger house and the halls are a little longer than in the previous house, which can be a good or bad thing, depending on the amount of speed my son can pick up. After a couple of harmless incidents, even our cat has learned to stay out of the way of moving children.

With two boys, I've learned things move fast—including bodies, bicycles, soccer balls, and even toys flying through the air. I wish overcoming grief followed the same plan of action.

My mother died a few months ago, leaving a gaping hole in her grandsons' hearts. Finding the words to explain why she's gone doesn't come easy for me, and the pain seems to settle in and take over on occasion.

So many times our children face struggles at school, hard times with their friends, a separation or divorce, or the loss of a grandparent, and peace eludes us all. Wrapping our kids up in our arms helps for a little while, but sometimes the pain returns and weighs heavy on their hearts.

Life would be easier if we could run down to the store, pick up a bucket of peace for a few dollars, divvy it out to our kids, and sit back and rest. But it would eventually run out again.

Thankfully, we don't have to turn into an explorer and search for peace. God sent his Son to give us lasting peace. In the few moments my 7 and 9 year old have been sitting still, we've learned some Bible verses and closed our eyes for prayer. In that time, peace washes over us and we know that God will continue to follow through on his promises and get us through the not-so-peaceful times.

| Julie Pollitt |

Action Step:

Take a moment to sit down together and read a Bible verse about peace. Continue to recite it for a while until everyone can remember it…and when the tough times return, know that peace is only a verse or a prayer away.

> **"Children are a gift from the Lord; they are a reward from him."**
>
> —Psalm 127:3

When my youngest child and only daughter celebrated her 18th birthday, I found myself feeling sentimental and reflective. My baby girl was officially an adult, and this mamma's nest was about to be empty.

My daughter hurriedly emerged from her room that morning, pounding out a rhythmic beat with her feet as she glided down the stairs. "No time for breakfast, Mom. I'll grab something at school." She quickly hugged my neck, grabbed her car keys, and walked out the door looking all grown-up in her cardigan sweater and smartly-tied scarf.

I felt a tear roll slowly down my cheek while I watched from the front window as she got into her car, started it up, and backed out of the driveway. Where had the years gone? It seemed like just a few months earlier she had regularly sobbed hysterically and locked her arms tightly around my neck when I dropped her off at preschool.

Throughout her 18 years of growing and learning and becoming, I had juggled motherhood and ministry and work. As I stood there in my eerily quiet house that November morning, I had to admit to myself that there had been times over the years when I had overcommitted myself in ministry or was distracted during family time by work responsibilities. I found myself wishing I'd spent a little less time working and a few more quiet mornings at home with nowhere to go and no appointments on my calendar.

It's a Good Thing Children Are a Treasure...They've Broken All My Other Ones

My girl was 18 years old. She would soon be heading off to college. I was thrilled for her. To this day, I am overjoyed at the personal nature of her relationship with her Lord. She is fabulously secure and wonderfully adventurous. But as I watched my daughter's car drive slowly out of sight on her 18th birthday, I longed to turn back the clock and spend more time just being, and playing, and enjoying my children.

As I wipe a tear, I encourage you to diligently guard your time with your children. Yes, serve God with passion in your local church or ministry. If you need to work, do so diligently, but treasure and guard your time with your children. One day, far sooner than you can ever imagine, you will be wiping tears from your eyes as you celebrate your youngest child's 18th birthday, wondering how she could possibly be all grown up. Time is short.

| Mindy Ferguson |

Action Step:

Today when you are at home with your children, make a conscious effort to take at least five minutes to just be with each child in his or her space. Give your full attention. Ask God to enable you to block out the stresses and demands of your day and to help you be fully present and engaged with your child. Your time with your children is a gift.

Why Does a Mommy Love Her Child?

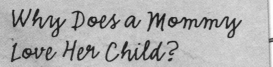

> **"Can a mother forget her nursing child? Can she feel no love for the child she has borne? But even if that were possible, I would not forget you!"**
>
> —Isaiah 49:15

I asked a preschooler, "Why does your mommy love you?" He said, "Because that's my mommy's job. Mommies love kids, and my mommy is really good at her job. Daddy wants her job to be cleaning the kitchen, but she really is not that good at that one."

Everyone has a job in this world that shows you are interested in someone. If you are a banker, you are interested in people who are investors. If you are a doctor, you are interested in people who are patients. If you are a researcher, you are interested in people who can be a statistic.

If you are a mother, you are interested in your child. You have other things you must do and care for, but your love for your child is the most important part of being a mother. You want your child to be the best he or she can be. Love allows you to accept a child who is different from you. Love allows you to accept a child who looks you in the face and says, "No! I will *not* do that!" Love allows you to pick up countless little toys off the floor when you are tired and sweep crumbs in areas you never thought food was allowed. Love allows you never to forget your child. Love even can allow a dirty kitchen to be less important than a child.

The job description of loving a child is the biggest one a person will ever have. It is through that love that the child is truly formed. A baby may be physically formed in a mother's womb, but he or she is emotionally formed while in a mother's presence. That is a job that is truly more important than cleaning a kitchen.

| Sheila Halasz |

Action Step:

Draw a big heart on a piece of paper, and display it in your kitchen today. Write either the names of your children in it, or write your mother's name in the heart. Pray that the people in your heart feel the love you have for them. If you can, show the heart to someone and share how very important the job of being a loving mother is and that it lasts a lot longer than a clean kitchen.

Jesus in a Tutu

> **"God blesses those who patiently endure testing and temptation. Afterward they will receive the crown of life that God has promised to those who love him."**
>
> —James 1:12

"I've fallen to my knees, Lord. I beg you to heal my baby. Please don't take her from me. Don't you hear my prayers to ease her pain, my fear, and my family's sorrow? I regret that milestones are passing both my girls without praises and joy. Countless hours, days, and months are being spent in multiple hospitals and visits to specialists, all without answers. I'm consumed in the unknown. Have you forsaken us? Lord, I cry out in desperation..."

My prayer ends abruptly by sweet singing. My older daughter twirls into the room. My heart melts at the sight of her. Her angelic smile is glowing. She leaps and sings innocently. She is adorned in the shiniest crown, ballet slippers, and a mighty purple tutu. She has topped her sublime ensemble with an oversized T-shirt of Jesus holding a barbell with the word "STRENGTH" across the bottom.

She twirls around me as she places the crown on my head, and the feeling of love and peace surrounds me. "Your Majesty," she says as she offers out her hand. My thoughts drift to Jesus. Only the comfort from our Savior can give us that feeling. An overwhelming joy fills my heart as I tell her she looks like "Jesus in a tutu." We both giggle and dance hand in hand as tears fill my eyes. I think to myself: This beautiful child has restored my heart today. In the midst of our storm, she exudes patience, grace, and joy. The attention focused on these trials hasn't broken her tender, loving spirit.

The face of Jesus will show up when you call upon him. He will shine through in many different forms. We need to open our eyes to see him. Questions arise that we can't answer ourselves. How can we trust God's plans? How can something good come out of tragedy? How can these trials refine my family and me? Look to the Bible for truth—stop the worrying, the doubting, and be mindful of the blessings that surround us.

God's got great things planned in our lives and for eternity. Persevere through the struggles. Find the hope in what lies in front of you. If we get lost in the misery of our problems and allow them to be obstacles in our faith, then we will surely miss seeing Jesus in a tutu.

| Janine Hamilton Stone |

Action Step:

If you've been struggling with something for a while, ask God to show you the blessings that are hidden within it. Those blessings will help you endure the pain and suffering that life is giving you. Pray for strength to persevere through this time. Today meditate for a few minutes on God's love. In those quiet moments, visualize Jesus offering a crown to you, his beloved princess.

Get together with one or two moms you know. Take time to talk about which of the devotions you've read recently was most meaningful to you and why. It's okay if you're all at different places in the book—just share what God puts on your heart.

Also, share an area of your life where you could use some prayer. Jot down what others say so you can remember to pray for them this week.

_____

_____

_____

_____

_____

While you're together, brainstorm a random act of kindness you can do right now. Write and address a card to someone who is lonely. Offer water to a worker outdoors. Whatever it is, do it now!

Mom Time!

Here's something fun to do with your family.

Quarter Walk

To change up your evening walks, take a quarter along. When you come to an intersection, let the coin determine where you'll go. You might say, "Heads, we turn right; tails, we turn left." Or, "Heads means we go straight, and tails means we turn around and go the other way." Kids take turns choosing the options and flipping the coin. You may end up on some long, rambling walks, but you're sure to laugh at how you go in circles!

Thimbleful of Blessing

"So she did as she was told. Her sons kept bringing jars to her, and she filled one after another. Soon every container was full to the brim!"

—2 Kings 4:5-6

I had an "aha!" moment the other day. I was in the car with the kids and we were listening to a recording of Bible stories. One was about the widow who was in debt and came to Elisha for help (2 Kings 4). Her husband had died and she couldn't pay her debts, so a creditor was going to take her two sons. Elisha asks her what she has at home. She responds that she has a little oil. So he tells her to go borrow jars from her neighbors, "as many as you can." The oil from her jar fills all the other jars and she sells it to pay her debt and lives on the rest of the money.

The question that ran across my mind as I was listening to this was: If I were in that situation, how many jars would I have borrowed? What if I looked silly or God didn't show up? Would I be willing to knock on doors all over town, or would I just borrow the neighbor's measuring cup? The amount of blessing the widow received was directly related to her faith in the situation. The oil ran until every jar was filled…and then it stopped. In my life, do I miss the bigness of some of God's blessings because my faith limits the outcome? Do I come to God with a prayer and a thimble asking him to fill it?

And for me, same as for the widow, there is a risk. What if I ask for big things or to see God move in big ways and don't get it? I trust that God is good and that he can give in abundance—but that doesn't mean he always will. There's a risk to ask and be told "no," "not now," or "yes, but not how you envision it." It is a risk to trust that God is who he says he is and will do things in his own time and for my good.

That's hard. But I'm practicing. Practicing my posture of opening my arms wide and saying, "Gimme! Gimme more of you, God. Gimme more evidence of your Spirit working in me. Show me your blessings and your work!" Then I wait. I wait knowing that God is good, that relationship with him is worth the risk, that he has bigger things planned for me than I could ever imagine.

> **"That is what the Scriptures mean when they say, 'No eye has seen, no ear has heard, and no mind has imagined what God has prepared for those who love him.'"**
>
> —1 Corinthians 2:9

| Sylvia Miller |

Action Step:

Take out a measuring cup, and put it someplace you will see it. As you come across it, ask God for the faith to see more of him in your day.

> **"We love each other because he loved us first."**
> —1 John 4:19

Last Easter, I woke to a peaceful house and a wide-awake 1-year-old. During our quiet morning together, I thought about how our lives had changed over the last year and I was reminded of the Savior who came to earth to redeem me of my sins.

You see, a year ago this time, my husband and I were the foster parents of two precious girls. They were our world before they reunited with their birth mother. A piece of my heart was missing when they left and a brick of self-protection went up around my emotions. I was left to wonder whether or not that one year we had with them was significant in their young lives.

That morning, I discovered that it was not only significant in their mortal lives, but their eternal lives as well. For that morning, while reaching to open the refrigerator door, I found a letter from our youngest foster daughter. She loves writing letters, and as an Easter present my husband and I—my husband whom they still affectionately call "dad" whenever we get the privilege of visits—bought her a journal with a fancy pencil. A piece of paper, torn from her journal, was stuck to the refrigerator by a magnet. It read as follows:

Dear Jesus,

I will worship you for who you are. I will worship you for who you are because you are spirit in the Holy God because you are our Savioer in the name of Jesus Crist I love you God you really are the savier of our whole life. I know you will always help us and always pertect us forever Jesus Christ and I know even if were bad we stll love us all.

I love you Jesus Christ.

(Misspellings reflect her 2nd grade knowledge ☺)

Even though this letter was not titled to me, it was all the same. Jesus came to save and "pertect" us from our sins and no matter what we do, we can never take his love from us. This morning not only do I know that I made a difference in her life, but I know that she has impacted my life and faith in ways that continue to help me understand the love of my Father in heaven.

| Shelley Lake |

Action Step:

Today, find an empty jar or vase and write the names of the people whom God has allowed you to love. Whenever you feel discouraged, take out that jar and pray over the names as you read through them.

The Not So Quiet Room

> "Be quiet and know that I am God. I will be honored among the nations. I will be honored in the earth."
>
> —Psalm 46:10, New Life Version

Raising two boys three years apart was challenging at times—but also rewarding. It seemed I spent most of my mom time being a referee. They even called me at work long distance to settle disputes.

Both boys played sports depending on which season it was. During the week, my husband and I rushed home from work to take them to their practices. They had different practice schedules and youth group on Wednesday nights, which pretty much took up the whole work week. Then Saturdays were game days. A lot of times the boys had games in different towns, which meant we each took one and went our separate ways.

After practices and games, there was meal preparation, dish washing, laundry, and whatever else needed to be done. Sundays, we attended church, and then the cycle started all over again.

Our house and yard seemed to always be filled with their friends. We enjoyed them and were happy they felt welcomed at our home. That also meant we knew where our boys were. However, there were times I thought if I heard "Mom" one more time I would scream.

Sometimes, when all the work was done, friends went home, and we settled down to watch television, I retreated to the quiet room to read a book or just meditate. Almost always, a few minutes into my retreat, one of the boys came in to have Mom all to himself. We talked about whatever was on his mind—school, sports, friends. As my sons got older, girls occupied the conversation. The quiet room was not so quiet now, and this was when I closed and laid down my book to listen to what they had to say.

| Beverly Fraizer |

Action Step:

God tells us to be quiet and know he is God. It can be difficult to be quiet with the crazy, hectic schedules most of us have. Today, be quiet not only to know God but also to hear what your children have to say. Give them one-on-one time. You never know when God might speak to you through them.

> **"Don't be afraid, for I am with you. Don't be discouraged, for I am your God. I will strengthen you and help you. I will hold you up with my victorious right hand."**
>
> —Isaiah 41:10

My grandmother used to call me a work widow. She likened my situation to her own when my grandfather was in the war, overseas, and communication was scarce. While my husband is not in the military or out of the country, his demanding job can keep him away from home for a week at a time. Other times, he arrives home only to sleep and shower. This is not the life I envisioned with him.

Late one night during a particularly grueling schedule, I sat on my bed, yellow lamplight shining on my open Bible, and cried out to God. Overwhelmed, isolated, and exhausted, my fears of being alone forever loomed over me. Hot tears slipped down my cheeks as I fought to still my sobs. I could hardly handle the load of pseudo-single parenting during the light of day, and far less would I be able to stand two toddlers awake at midnight.

My attempts to quiet my crying were unsuccessful. Shortly, two little feet pattered into my room and my daughter rubbed her eyes in the dim light. She held her arms out to me. Would I let her sleep with me tonight, or would I stick to the routine and force her to go back to her own bed?

Studying her tousled hair and round, sleep-blushed face, my heart calmed. I brushed the wetness from my chin and held the covers back for her. Snuggling together, smelling the lavender bath wash from her hair, I felt the tenderhearted mercy of the Lord. Yes, I would likely have to break this co-sleeping habit again and again, but for now I could afford to take comfort from the warmth of my child. I could let my heart rest in his promise to hold us all, including my husband as he worked away from home. My children would not suffer unduly from the love and acceptance of occasionally sleeping in my too-empty bed.

My husband still works away from home more often than I would like. It's not quite the life I planned, but this struggle cannot compare with the peace of relying on Jesus for strength and wisdom. When I treat myself with kindness, my relationship with God, with my children, and even with my husband grows stronger. Work widow, single parent, or otherwise, the great I AM is with us. He will give us strength in all things.

| Shelley Ring |

Action Step:

Be kind to yourself today. Find a comfortable spot and record one or more of God's promises on paper, and then commit it to memory. When life challenges you, speak his promise out loud.

Mom to Mom 5

Get together with one or two moms you know. Take time to talk about which of the devotions you've read recently was most meaningful to you and why. It's okay if you're all at different places in the book—just share what God puts on your heart.

Also, share an area of your life where you could use some prayer. Jot down what others say so you can remember to pray for them this week.

_____

_____

_____

_____

_____

What YouTube videos make you laugh the hardest? Show one or two of your favorites to each other and enjoy a hearty belly laugh. (It's great exercise for your abs!)

Mom Time!

Here's something fun to do with your family.

Water Fight

While your kids are at school or anywhere but home, make a bunch of water balloons. Put them in a bucket or laundry basket, and set this on your front porch. Include a big note that says, "These are for you. I'm waiting out back with the hose!" Then actually wait out back with the water hose—and let the water fun begin!

Fire Alarm

> **"Never stop praying."**
> —1 Thessalonians 5:17

Upstairs, changing yet another messy diaper, I heard my oldest daughter yell from downstairs, "Mom, the fire alarm is going off!"

"Again? Already?" I groaned inwardly as I finished changing the baby. I was in no hurry to head downstairs. A mother of six children (five at home) certainly does not need a fire alarm going off to add excitement to her day.

Fortunately, the "fire alarm" in our house is a small digital alarm I set each time I add wood to the fireplace, to beckon me back at the time I expect to need to add more wood. During icy weather, the alarm noisily calls me every 45 to 65 minutes. However, regularly stoking the fire with a lot of wood is necessary to maintain a physically comfortable home for my family.

Whether a home uses wood, gas, or electricity for heat, icy weather demands frequent, intense effort to keep the home comfortably warm. In like manner, our often over-taxed mothers' spirits need frequent nourishment from our Lord to maintain the warm, loving demeanor of Jesus. Maintaining an open line of communication with God throughout our day is absolutely necessary for this. First Thessalonians 5:17 instructs us to "never stop praying."

We can't walk around all day with our hands folded, heads bowed, and eyes closed. That would be dangerous. Thankfully, that's not what the verse means. What it does mean is that to maintain a healthy spirit, we need to keep an open line of communication with God. As we speak, we can remember that God hears us, and we can be ready to take his guidance. It's like calling someone on the phone and never hanging up. You are more self-conscious and act better, knowing they hear every word you say. You're also extraordinarily more confident, knowing their wisdom is so quickly and easily there for you to access.

| Lori Schmidtke |

Action Step:

Throughout today, each time you stoke your fire, or hear your air conditioner or heater turn on to maintain the level of comfort in your home for your physical body, hear God beckon. Pray and make sure you are maintaining your open line of communication with God, who abundantly provides for your spirit.

Walking on Water (When You're in Over Your Head)

> "But when [Peter] saw the strong wind and the waves, he was terrified and began to sink. 'Save me, Lord!' he shouted. Jesus immediately reached out and grabbed him. 'You have so little faith,' Jesus said. 'Why did you doubt me?'"
> —Matthew 14:30-31

I was determined to do things "better" this pregnancy. Both before and after the birth of my second daughter, I found myself drowning in depression. But with my third daughter, I was convinced things could be different. The third time's the charm, right?

And things were downright charming for the first 18 weeks. I had my healthy diet plan, my exercise routine, a vitamin regime down pat, and I felt like Supermom. Until one day I started crying and couldn't stop. I spent weeks sobbing on my kitchen floor.

Instead of promptly reaching out for help, I stubbornly refused to accept that I was in this place. Again. I was embarrassed. After all, shouldn't I know how to beat this thing by now? I tried to deny that I was sinking at all. And when the waves of depression swept over my head, I tried to convince myself that I'm a really good swimmer.

But a dear friend once told me it doesn't matter how great a swimmer I am; I will never be able to swim to China.

When Peter similarly became overwhelmed by the literal waves around him, he temporarily took his eyes off Jesus and promptly began to sink. But despite his momentary lack of faith, Peter chose to immediately call out to the only One who could save him. Yet here I was, trying desperately to claw my way back to the boat all by myself. I wasn't merely sinking; I was drowning.

It was time for me to follow Peter's lead, to cry out, "Save me, Lord!" and to place my hand firmly into Jesus', even as the storm raged on.

For now, we're still out in the middle of that restless sea, Jesus and me. I'm still anxious about what things will be like after my daughter is born. But as long as my hand is in his, I no longer doubt that we will make it back safely into the boat and into the calm, one step on the water at a time.

| Karen Neumair |

Action Step:

What storm is threatening to sink you or your family today? Pray a one-sentence prayer that you will stop merely treading water but instead firmly grip the pierced hands of Jesus. Write your prayer on a piece of paper or notecard, and tape it inside the cupboard where you keep cups or glasses so you'll see it often.

Stuck in a Cave

> **"I cry out to God Most High, to God who will fulfill his purpose for me."**
>
> —Psalm 57:2

The moment David felt the trickle of warm oil against his scalp must have been memorable. Out of all his brothers—even all of Israel's young men—God chose him to be anointed by Samuel to lead his people as king.

Now here in Psalm 57, we find the king-to-be huddled in a cave, pursued by the very man God intended him to replace. The plan doesn't seem to be working out so well, does it? Yet David, surely more than a little preoccupied with his physical safety, spends 9 out of 11 verses praising God. Verse 2 stands out in particular:

I cry out to God Most High, to God who will fulfill his purpose for me.

Really? Saul's pursuit seems contrary to God's purposes.

I was stuck in a cave recently. My 18-year-old son, already saddled with three serious auto-immune conditions, became dangerously ill. Month after month, his already thin frame grew thinner, and his exhaustion curtailed his ability to attend college classes. Yet God had called him to the mission field as a nurse. How would God fulfill that promise if my son's college career was stalled?

Perhaps you're in a similar type of cave. A claustrophobic prison, reminding you of the fresh-air promises you once clung to. The fetid air and ominous footfalls of the enemy nearby are a constant reminder that God did not come through. Your cave might be one of physical exhaustion from the myriad demands of motherhood, emotional fatigue due to a rocky marriage, or the burden of crushing debt.

How different would David's character have been if he hadn't endured hardship? If everything promised had come easily? I wonder if he might have ended up more like Saul. It was likely that times like these in the cave, not knowing how God was ever going to keep his promises, were the ones that shaped David into the king God desired for his people—and a man after God's own heart.

If you find yourself in a cave of emotion or circumstances, take David's prescription. He acknowledged his situation. He didn't live in denial. But he focused his thoughts on what God had done and what God would do, and praised him even though he couldn't see the solution. He expected God to act. Verse 3 says, "My God will send forth his unfailing love and faithfulness."

God will fulfill his purposes, and our cave experiences are part of the process.

| Debbie M. Allen |

Action Step:

Many worship songs are based on psalms. When you're feeling stuck in your cave, sing one that you like (or another praise song), and picture David exalting God in the middle of his trials.

A Bad Case of Momnesia

"Show mercy and kindness to one another."
—Zechariah 7:9

It happened. Oh, it wasn't going to happen to me, but it happened. How could I ever be such a crazy woman, to get this mixed up?

I stood at the counter, waiting to check my bags for our trip to visit my parents, two kids in tow. My husband had dropped us by the airport on his way to work, and we were off for an adventure.

"I'm sorry, ma'am, you don't have a reservation." The attendant looked at me blankly.

"There must be some explanation. Can you please check again?" I asked, pawing through my purse for the illusive printout of our reservation, a measure of irritation creeping into my already frazzled mind.

After what seemed like forever, he said, "Oh, here you are. Your flight left yesterday."

As the realization of what he had just said sank into my brain, I did what any self-respecting mom would do. I burst into tears!

Did he have any idea how hard I had worked just to get to this point? Did he know that packing, rearranging music lessons, getting the laundry done so my husband wouldn't run out of socks while we were gone, and just getting myself dressed and ready while trying to keep my kids from killing each other in the craziness, was almost more than I could do? Did he know that the reason we were even going on this trip was because my mom was dying of cancer?

He had a lot of nerve, telling me that I'd missed my flight. By a whole day. Gently, the supervisor who had come up behind the bewildered attendant spoke to me. "Let's see what we can do," she said. She politely took over the computer from the poor guy who had only been the deliverer of truth, and in a few minutes she said, "We actually do have room on today's flight, and I'll waive the change fee."

Once again, I cried! Thanking her profusely through my tears, I thought how kind it was of God to put her in my day. "Thank you, Jesus," I breathed.

I've had several other cases of "momnesia." I'll probably have more. But that day, in that moment, another mom did what she could to make my day bearable, and it has inspired me to extend grace to other moms who, on occasion, need it when their momnesia kicks in.

| DeeAnn Bragaw |

Action Step:

Take a moment and think about your worst case of "momnesia." Can you laugh about it yet? Thank God for his patient kindness, and ask him to show you someone to whom you can give grace today.

Get together with one or two moms you know. Take time to talk about which of the devotions you've read recently was most meaningful to you and why. It's okay if you're all at different places in the book—just share what God puts on your heart.

Also, share an area of your life where you could use some prayer. Jot down what others say so you can remember to pray for them this week.

_____

_____

_____

_____

_____

What's a worship song that gets you through the day? Play a song for your mom friends—you can sing it or play it from your phone or other device. Encourage each other with music and a moment of praising God.

Mom Time!

Here's something fun to do with your family.

Lunch Swap

About once a month, announce that your kids need to pack lunch for one another. Set parameters for foods that are healthy—but encourage them to also be fun and creative and include a special treat for their sibling. It's fun to see your children write notes and draw special pictures on napkins for one another. And, bonus...you get a break! If you're brave, invite your kids to pack your lunch as well!

All Alone

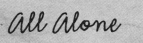

> **"So now I am giving you a new commandment: Love each other. Just as I have loved you, you should love each other. Your love for one another will prove to the world that you are my disciples."**
>
> —John 13:34-35

"Did you have a good day at school?" I asked as Lindsey burst through the door.

"It was all right," she said. "But the whole class got in trouble, because everyone was talking. And nobody played with me at recess."

"I'm sorry," I said, hugging her.

"Actually," Lindsey added, "no one ever plays with me. Every day I play on the monkey bars all alone."

My heart broke for her. Lindsey is a great kid, and I want every other child in her school to know that. I want them to invite her to play with them. I want Lindsey to be loved not only by her family, but by her classmates. And they do like her. They just don't reach out to her.

Lindsey and I talked about some things she can do if she wants someone to play with during recess. As we talked, I realized that God, too, wants his children—you and me—to be accepted. He wants all of us to treat each other lovingly and to build a community with each other.

Yet sometimes even we Christians fail to reach out and invite each other into our inner circles. We probably don't do it on purpose, but this fact still leaves some people playing alone anyway. And just like my heart hurts when Lindsey plays alone, God's heart hurts when his children have to play alone.

That's why God told us to love one another. This love that he commanded was to be so extraordinary that by it the world would know that we were his. It's not an easy love to extend, but it's the kind of love God wants. And it's the kind of love he offers each one of us, every single moment of our lives.

God never leaves us to play alone. And he doesn't want us to leave each other to have to play alone either.

| Megan Breedlove |

Action Step:

Take a few moments to think about someone to whom you can reach out today. It could be by doing something as simple as writing an email or making a phone call, or as elaborate as taking him or her out to a spontaneous lunch.

Kindergarten's Empty Nest

> "So don't worry about tomorrow, for tomorrow will bring its own worries. Today's trouble is enough for today."
>
> —Matthew 6:34

Some of my friends were recently talking about watching their children head off to college. A range of comments sprinkled into the mix, including sighs of relief now that they've done their job getting Junior off to the big leagues, and sadness at the now-empty nests.

On occasion, I wonder what life will be like once my kids are out of the house. Even though they are still in elementary school, I look off in the far distance—well, the other side of the room—and picture life with an empty nest. Tears well up, a flood of emotions start caving in, and the tissues come flying out of the box.

I'll never forget my son's first day of kindergarten. I feared he'd cry the entire day without me, not make any friends, and never be able to find his way to the car circle at the end of the day. After all, he'd spent almost every waking moment by my side. How could he possibly survive without me?

But, at the end of the day, he was first in line at the car circle, jumped right into the car, and chatted the entire ride home about meeting new friends and learning all about school. He even shared his excitement about returning the next day. I realized I needed him as much as he needed me.

When my younger son started elementary school, I got a twinge of the empty nest syndrome while my children were away for the day. My heart pumped with worry for a while, but I soon realized God was already teaching me early on what life will one day be like when they leave for college and then head off to start their own lives.

| Julie Pollitt |

Action Step:

Take some time with your kids. Tuck games away, put chores on hold, and head outdoors. Enjoy a walk around the block or riding bikes. Embrace each moment together.

Are You Thankful?

> "Be thankful in all circumstances, for this is God's will for you who belong to Christ Jesus."
>
> —1 Thessalonians 5:18

I asked a preschooler, "What are you thankful for?" He said, "I don't know what thankful is, but I know "thank full" is better than "thank empty.""

Everyone is thankful about something, and everyone is ungrateful about something. It's up to us to draw the lines where we want to be. Anything we look at can be seen through a lens of gratefulness or ungratefulness. You can choose to be more full or more empty.

The line in the grocery store can be seen as a frustrating waste of time, or it can be seen as an opportunity to spend time in thought and be grateful for shelves so full of food.

The lack of sleep from a crying baby can be seen as wear and tear on a day and a reason to breed crabbiness, or it can be seen as a night that no one else in the entire world will ever get to experience. It can be a night where a young child is loved in a way that no one else would ever love him. It is a night where the safety of a warm house, ample water and food, and the dawn of a new day can bring overwhelming gratitude.

The guy who cuts you off in traffic can be seen as adjectives that fingers should not type on a keyboard. He can be a cause for raised blood pressure and revenge. This same guy can be seen as a way to get your attention and be grateful you have the physical ability to maneuver a car. Many do not. Only a small percentage of the world's population even owns a car, and you are one of that small privileged percentage.

When God asks us to be thankful in all circumstances, he wants us to be truly full and never fully empty.

| Sheila Halasz |

Action Step:

Fill a glass of water only half full. Imagine yourself very thirsty and thank God for the water. Are you thanking him for what is there? Or focusing on what's missing? What can you do to concentrate on the fullness of thanks and not the emptiness?

> **"Every word of God proves true. He is a shield to all who come to him for protection."**
>
> —Proverbs 30:5

From the moment our children are born, our instinct is to protect them. We want the best for them. We want to shield them from the cruelties of the world. We want to wrap them in a blanket and swaddle them and keep them close forever. Yet as they grow older, we know we have to loosen that blanket and let them become the people God intended.

As soon as I knew I was expecting until this very day, I have been quilting a blanket of prayer for each of my children. I know God loves them even more than I ever could. Thus, I know my prayers for protection and guidance will not be in vain.

One of my sons taught me how precious prayer for him is and the peace it can bring. As a captain in the Army, his unit was being sent overseas, off to war. I have no words to describe the fear I had. If I could, I would have gladly gone in his place. This Mommy wanted her boy home, on friendly soil. As he prepared to leave, I realized the best thing I could do for him was pray. A good friend reminded me that the same God who was protecting him here at home would protect him no matter where he was in the world. The peace those words gave me is immeasurable.

Of course, every time I heard a news report of a young man losing his life or being injured, I wept, but I also gave thanks that it was not my son whose name was reported in the newspaper. Prayer is what kept me going, and my son told me more times than I can count how he felt the prayers so many were extending on his behalf.

Whether your child is heading off to his first sleepover, off to college, or off to war, wrap your child in a blanket of prayer. The peace it brings will change both of your lives.

| Jennifer Nystrom |

Action Step:

Start a prayer journal for your child. Record your prayers and praises for them. Keep a record of the things God has done for them through prayer.

Get together with one or two moms you know. Take time to talk about which of the devotions you've read recently was most meaningful to you and why. It's okay if you're all at different places in the book—just share what God puts on your heart.

Also, share an area of your life where you could use some prayer. Jot down what others say so you can remember to pray for them this week.

_____

_____

_____

_____

_____

It's likely you're a thrifty mom who enjoys both giving and receiving hand-me-downs for your kids. But what about you? See if the other moms you gather with are willing to do a purse or scarf or other accessory trade. Bring along a few accessories you don't use anymore, and see if someone else can find joy and a bit of color for her wardrobe from them.

Mom Time!
Here's something fun to do with your family.

What Color Is It?

Select a color at random. Go shopping with the kids and pick out food items only of that color to prepare for a fun meal. If the foods you find are new to you, you might need to look online for recipes to use. The same color place cards and table settings can join the fun as well. Fun conversations are centered on the color and the shopping experience. As a variation, collect specific-color food items you already have.

Longing for Less

> **"I wait quietly before God, for my victory comes from him. He alone is my rock and my salvation, my fortress where I will never be shaken."**
>
> —Psalm 62:1-2

I've been thinking about how hectic and crazy the pace of life has become. How, I'm sure, God never designed us to handle the stress levels we're carrying every day. We cook, clean, and do most of the shopping. We chauffeur the kids to games, to practices, to lessons, school, play dates, church groups. I could go on and on. We counsel and maintain relationships with our husbands, friends, families, churches, neighbors, and in-laws. Maybe you volunteer at your kids' school, at your church, in the community. Maybe you have a job outside of the home as well. Forget hobbies! All while being sure to present our flawless, photo-shopped best on social media. I'm tired just reading this!

Many of us moms keep such a frantic pace that we lose sight of the important things. We grow too busy for the very thing we need. The very one and only way we can do the impossible. Standing in the middle of the schedule, the chaos, and yes, in the storm, is Jesus…The One. He is not stressed or afraid. He's waiting for you to remember that he IS God. And in our efforts to juggle it all, with 50 balls in the air, deep down inside we know we cannot do this. We need a Savior. We need his perspective. We need God to set our priorities and help us let go of the things we do not need, the things our kids do not need. To bring us back to what we cannot live without—God's presence in our everyday. And when we invite him into the details, he is glorified.

I long for simplicity. Simply to love my family, serve my God, and be happy and content. To live in continual gratitude...not wanting or striving. I long to be still and know. Lord, please touch all who read this and feel a stir inside, as their spirits cry out for less.

| Corissa I. Snyder |

Action Step:

Today, put a worship song on that you love and wait quietly before God. Listen to the music with your eyes closed so you won't be distracted. Ask Jesus to speak to your heart as you quiet yourself before the Lord and invite him into your day.

"Rapped" in Peace

> "Don't worry about anything; instead, pray about everything. Tell God what you need, and thank him for all he has done. Then you will experience God's peace, which exceeds anything we can understand."
>
> —Philippians 4:6-7

There is nothing better than sharing in a "God Moment" with your child. You know, a time when it is undeniable that God was with you, anticipated your need, and provided just what you needed, at just the right time.

When my daughter was 10 years old, she was having some health issues. The doctor wanted her to have an MRI, which meant that she had to remain perfectly still for over an hour while lying in the machine. We talked about activities she could do to assist her in keeping still during the test. The day came for the test. I was able to sit next to her as she lay in the MRI machine. She decided to have me read her a book. The technician informed us that the first session was about ready to begin. I started to read and watched as my daughter remained perfectly still.

Twenty minutes passed, and then I heard over the intercom "We are done with the first session. Are you ready to start the next session?" My daughter looked at me with tears streaming down her face. I asked the technician if we could take a break, and after exiting the machine, my daughter said to me, "I can't go back, Mommy." We proceeded to pray together, and I asked, "God, please help Becca relax and be able to complete the test so we can get her better. It would be so great if you could even help her fall asleep." We went back into the MRI room, and I asked what she wanted to do. She said, "I think I want to listen to Toby Mac." I told the technician, who put the music in the player. The technician gave me a funny look as she listened to the rap music my daughter had chosen. Becca settled in, and just a few minutes into this session I could hear her breathing become slow and deep. "Could she be asleep?" I thought. Sure enough, she was sleeping while listening to the upbeat rap music she had chosen.

To this day, my daughter and I talk about this event which was such a direct answer to our specific prayer. Experiencing the power of God is life-changing and serves to fuel our faith as we face the challenges of life. I am so thankful that God hears the cries of our hearts and shows us his overwhelming love.

| Leslie J. Smith |

Action Step:

Honestly pour your heart out to God and ask specifically for what you need. If you have a prayer journal, write your prayer and date it so you can review this as time goes by as a reminder of what God is doing in your life. And if you, like Becca, enjoy rap music, turn it up today!

Let Them Eat... Cupcakes!

> "But Jesus said, 'Let the children come to me. Don't stop them! For the Kingdom of Heaven belongs to those who are like these children.'"
> —Matthew 19:14

Yesterday, my granddaughters Rylan (5) and Kinley (4) helped me make cupcakes for their cousin Christian's fifth birthday. Cooking is a big event when it's real and not in the let's-pretend, kid-sized kitchen. Aprons on, chairs to the counter, measuring cups out, all supplies ready, electric mixer plugged in, oven preheating.

There are certain steps that these two are always eager to do: lining the cupcake pan with colorful papers, squatting down to check that Grammy has measured ingredients to the correct line in the glass cup, slowly pouring the water and oil in the big bowl, taking a turn with the mixer (and licking leftover batter off the beaters, of course). But adding eggs? That's supposed to be Grammy Val's job. Nevertheless, I coaxed them into giving the old egg-cracking a try. Meticulous Rylan was willing to tap the egg on the metal bowl, but I had to finish the cracking and drop the raw egg into the cake mix, "because eggs are too messy." Kinley was up for the whole adventure. She tapped, she squished, egg ran over her hand, but she got it in the bowl.

Kinley proceeded to give me a slimy high five, and started woo-hooing and dancing around the kitchen, declaring, "I'm telling Mommy I cracked an egg by myself! Whew! I can crack eggs...I have the best life!"

How do we get back there? To those essential and elementary moments of discovery and joy—when we take chances and risk embarrassment to learn a new skill, when we realize that life is a beautiful gift, the best gift? Perhaps when life doesn't feel like it's all it's cracked up to be, God is prompting us to try something new. In Isaiah 11:6, the Bible tells us that, "a little child will lead them all," so maybe it's our children who are giving us the real cooking lesson for life.

| Valerie Turner |

Action Step:

Try a new recipe in your kitchen or do some work in your garden. Let all your senses take in how aromatic, beautiful, and wondrous life can be, and thank God for those moments of heaven on earth.

> **"They will be my people, and I will be their God. And I will give them one heart and one purpose: to worship me forever, for their own good and for the good of all their descendants. And I will make an everlasting covenant with them: I will never stop doing good for them. I will put a desire in their hearts to worship me, and they will never leave me."**
>
> —Jeremiah 32:38-40

When my four children were growing up, I wanted them to become Christians and be victorious. I assumed it would be pain-free for them. I discovered this passage in Jeremiah. What stood out in the passage was, "I will never stop doing good for them."

A few years ago, my youngest daughter's husband fell 25 feet from a climbing wall. I received a stunning phone message from my daughter saying, "I am sitting here alone in a chapel of the hospital and three teams of doctors are trying to save Justin's life." I reminded God of the verse... ending with, "I will never stop doing good for them," and prayed with our family and friends for his life. During those long hours before the doctors had the final report, I flew out to be with my daughter. I wondered what Justin's prognosis would be.

Justin broke his neck, his wrist, and his rib. It was a miracle he lived from that fall. I was reading in my Bible and God gave me a verse, which I handed to Justin: "Be at rest, O my soul, for the Lord has been good to you. For you, O Lord, have delivered my soul from death, my eyes from tears, my feet from stumbling, that I may walk before the Lord in the land of the living" (Psalm 116:7-9, New International Version).

God's promises are throughout the Bible. I learned young that we could claim them because God gave them to us to claim. These promises that have been true for me will be true for my children and grandchildren after me.

| Barbara Bereit |

Action Step:

When you hear a Bible verse shared at church or Sunday school, or when you are reading and see a verse that is a promise, write it down. Pray the verse back to God and ask him to fulfill his promise. Thank God ahead of time for what he will do to fulfill this promise from the Bible.

Mom to Mom 8

Get together with one or two moms you know. Take time to talk about which of the devotions you've read recently was most meaningful to you and why. It's okay if you're all at different places in the book—just share what God puts on your heart.

Also share an area of your life where you could use some prayer. Jot down what others say so you can remember to pray for them this week.

_____

_____

_____

_____

_____

Go for a walk together. If the weather's great, head to the park. If not, try a mall or gym or other place you can walk and talk.

Mom Time!

Here's something fun to do with your family.

My Favorite Food

For dinner or a special day (such as Thanksgiving), each person coming to the meal picks his or her favorite food. Only that food is served, even if these don't "go" together. Each person shares what about their choice makes it their favorite. When the meal is finished, the person who chose each food gets to keep the leftovers just for his or her enjoyment later in the day or week. One family shared that this meant they once had stuffed hot peppers, cherry pie, mashed potatoes with brown gravy, pecan pie, brie cheese, and smoked turkey with dressing. What will happen if you try this? Tacos, cupcakes, and chips? Give it a try!

Come to Me... I Know What to Do!

> "Then Jesus said, 'Come to me, all of you who
> are weary and carry heavy burdens, and I will
> give you rest.'"
>
> —Matthew 11:28

"Mommy, can you play with me? Mommy, can I have food? Mommy, why? But why? But why?"

"Chloe, mommy is trying to talk with Auntie Christy." I found myself yearning for every last moment with my friend from childhood, but as we sat in a small café New Year's Eve morning, we found ourselves very distracted. Between my 2-year-old daughter and my 10-week-old infant, the distractions were mounting.

"What was I saying?" Christy said.

"You know, I'm really not sure," I said with a smile, "Welcome to my life." As we sat there trying to pick up our conversation in pieces, I realized how distracted my life had become on a larger scale. Laundry, cleaning, cooking, shopping, work, and exercise. Somewhere in the mix, I would get time to say a quick prayer, but my spiritual life as a whole had definitely been put on the sidelines. It got me thinking—why do we allow these seemingly harmless day-to-day activities distract us from a deeper, more meaningful relationship with Jesus? Why are they suddenly more important than spending time with him each day? Whether you are a young mom or seasoned mother, I'm sure you can relate. When we stray away from deepening our relationship with God, we tend to go about life by ourselves. And that only lasts so long before we become weak and tired. One of my favorite verses in the Bible is Matthew 11:28: "Come to me, all of you who are weary and carry heavy burdens, and I will give you rest." Essentially, when we allow time for God each day, we are laying our burdens, distractions—or whatever you want to call them—at his feet. And by setting time aside each day for reading the Bible and praying, we are not only strengthening an eternal relationship, we are allowing ourselves healing and rest.

"I guess it wasn't that important," Christy shrugged and smiled at me as she took Chloe into her lap. "I am just glad we have the time together— that's what matters most."

| Heidi Guzman |

Action Step:

Wake up 10 minutes early tomorrow, and commit to spending time reading your Bible for those 10 minutes. Pray throughout your day (in the car, while you shower, while walking from one place to another, or while you do housework). He desperately wants to be with you no matter what you are doing!

A Change of Pants...I Mean, Heart

> **"You can make many plans, but the Lord's purpose will prevail."**
>
> —Proverbs 19:21

I can remember a time when I could remember things. I never had to ask myself questions like: Did I pay the electricity bill? Or when I was the last time I washed my hair? I used to be organized. My house was complimented often. And, not to brag, but people often told me how nice I smelled.

Then I had Nathan.

I can pinpoint exactly when it happened, this day the Neat-Clean-Great-at-Remembering-Things existence came to an end.

I was out shopping. I had baby Nathan in a wrap when I *felt* it more than I actually heard or smelled it. Explosion. From Nathan's nether regions.

There is never a good time for a diaper explosion, but in the middle of a store and wrapped in a Moby Wrap was definitely not the best time. I ran as fast as I could to the dressing room, untangled Nathan from the wrap and surveyed the damage.

It was everywhere. I mean, *everywhere*. I completely disrobed him until he was totally naked; I used every last wipe I had getting him cleaned off. I pulled out the extra outfit for Nathan I always carried with me, reached in the bag for a new diaper and...There. Were. None. Zilch. I had forgotten to put more diapers in the diaper bag.

That was the moment. I still remember standing there, panting, staring at my naked 2-month-old son who was giggling like this was the best fun he'd ever had, and realizing this motherhood thing wasn't for the weak at heart. Or the weak at stomach. I ripped that diaper bag apart searching for maybe one tiny diaper that got shoved in the wrong pocket. Nothing.

But I *did* find a maxi-pad. I'm not proud of what I did next but it had to be done. I looked at Nathan and before I could really even think about it, I slapped the pad right up against Nathan's you-know-what, buttoned his onesie over it, grabbed him, and ran out the door. By the time we got home, he'd peed through the pad, all over himself, and all through his clothes, and it soaked through his car seat.

I learned three things that day:
- I was never in control of my life and I certainly wasn't now.
- Just because things don't go the way I'm expecting doesn't mean God isn't working in the middle of them.
- I will never believe those commercials where they pour a gallon of blue water onto a maxi-pad and it doesn't leak ever again.

| Erynn Alaine O'Brien |

Action Step:

Think about a time when something in your life didn't go as planned—big or small. How did you handle it? How can you ask God to better prepare you for the next time plans change?

Messing Up Motherhood

> **"Direct your children onto the right path, and when they are older, they will not leave it."**
> —Proverbs 22:6

Motherhood is tough. I taught good housekeeping habits, yet my girls' rooms still looked like they had been hit by the storm of the century, not to mention that a whole colony of trolls could have survived undetected in their closets for years. I taught tangible ways to express thankfulness, yet many "thanks" for presents and kind gestures fell through the cracks. I taught the importance of seeking the presence of God and his wisdom in making decisions, but that practice fell by the wayside—in both small and big ways.

We don't always get to see the immediate results of our motherhood efforts. We won't see some of them in our lifetime. Plus, some of the things we thought were of paramount importance aren't. God knows what needs to be emphasized and what needs to be downplayed. He knows how to use each situation, whether it needs to be highlighted or downplayed.

As moms, we aren't big enough to mess up God's plans. It's prideful of us to think we can actually destroy what God has planned. Sure, we can create bumps in the road that later require detours, but we can't derail another person's life altogether. God's sovereign plan is much bigger and better than anything we can plan and imagine.

So why do we carry the weight of our children's future on our shoulders? What if we relaxed a bit, let ourselves make some mistakes, and in the process, let our children see how we need and fully rely on God for all guidance and provision? We know with our minds that God has simply loaned us the children in our care, so why don't we continually admit and live out that fact with our hearts? After all, as difficult as it is to imagine, God can and does love our children immeasurably more than we do. They are his.

| Susan Lawrence |

Action Step:

Look at photos of your children and consider how they resemble their heavenly Father. "Hand them over" to him in a tangible way, such as placing the photos in your Bible or other meaningful place in your home or car.

It's a Good Thing Children Are a Treasure…They've Broken All My Other Ones

Cabin Fever

> "He alone is my refuge, my place of safety; he is my God, and I trust him."
>
> —Psalm 91:2

Winter arrived early that year. Not to say that the Colorado snow flew early. No, this early winter was marked by more runny noses, nasty coughs, icky tummies, and feverish red faces than I had fingers to count on.

With two toddler boys, our home was scattered with board books, piles of dirty laundry, well-loved blankets, and Hot Wheels race cars. Oh—and a household petri dish where germs grew well and never went away. At times, we resigned ourselves to our bunkered-in condition and just accepted it with a sigh. Then there were times when we had watched one too many Tom and Jerry episodes, read one too many board books, and raced one too many cars down the winding race track. If something didn't happen—and soon—we were going to start climbing the walls. Cabin Fever had set in.

This is where it gets dangerous. We had been stuck in the house for days on end and the boys had that crazy combination of bored and feisty going on. I rationalize that we are not contagious anymore, and we certainly have picked up every germ known to mankind so the risks of leaving our home are pretty low…right? The next thing I know, I find myself driving to the mall play place with two very excited little boys. This was not just any mall play place. This was our favorite, complete with plastic bridge, slide, fort, and river!

As we drove, I listed off the reminders. Wash hands, followed by hand sanitizer. Cough into your elbow. Get a tissue if you need one. As we arrive at our prized destination, I thought I had covered it all. All the energy that had been contained exploded into little-boy play. I turned to put down all that a mom with toddlers travels with while my two young ones ripped off their shoes and socks. As I turned back around, I experienced one of those slow motion scenes when a mom desperately needs to stop her child from what he is going to do next, but has no way to get there in time. Sitting in the middle of the play place was my son, licking the bottoms of his feet. Yes...licking the bottoms of his feet. I watched in stunned horror. He calmly looked over at me and said, "Mom, if you don't lick, you don't stick." I smiled and sat down. I guess there are just some things a mom can't cover.

| Dawn Canny |

Action Step:

Being a mom is full of moments that are both in and out of your control. Blow a balloon up (in your control), let it go and watch it buzz around until it falls to the ground (out of your control). Thank God that he is always in control.

Get together with one or two moms you know. Take time to talk about which of the devotions you've read recently was most meaningful to you and why. It's okay if you're all at different places in the book—just share what God puts on your heart.

Also, share an area of your life where you could use some prayer. Jot down what others say so you can remember to pray for them this week.

_____

_____

_____

_____

_____

Take a photo of you and your mom friends. Print it and put it on your fridge right next to school pictures and handmade art. Pray for your friends this week, and thank God that you have them!

Mom Time!

Here's something fun to do with your family.

Window Darts

Too tired to play an active game–but your kids still have lots of energy? Use a bar of soap to draw targets on the largest window in your house. You can always wash it off later (like in a few months...). Use toy guns or bow and arrow toys that shoot suction darts. You can sit on the couch or lie on the bed and take turns shooting suction darts at the window targets. The kids get to retrieve the darts between rounds so you don't have to move!

Holding Hands

> "I will bless the Lord who guides me; even at night my heart instructs me. I know the Lord is always with me. I will not be shaken, for he is right beside me...You will show me the way of life, granting me the joy of your presence and the pleasures of living with you forever."
> —Psalm 16:7-8, 11

My young granddaughters were staying with me for an extended weekend. They don't live nearby, so this was a very special treat for all of us. We had many adventures as we explored the world together, but one of the sweetest moments for me was when I felt my granddaughter slip her warm hand in mine. She looked up at me and smiled and my heart was mush. I loved that she wanted to be near me. We laughed, skipped, and she heeded my encouragement to hold on tight when we crossed a busy street. She trusted me to keep her safe. There was no protest that she was too old to hold hands crossing the street. She wanted to stay near. Now that all my children are grown and out of the nest, this was a rare treat. I had forgotten what it felt like to walk hand in hand with a trusting young child.

When I reflect on that special time, I am reminded of my heavenly Father's desire to take me by the hand and walk with me through each day. What an amazing idea! God delights in my childlike grasp. I wonder, "Do I willingly stay near? Do I slip my hand in his and trust him to keep me?" Sometimes I find myself thinking I am too big to need help crossing the street, but my granddaughter's upturned face and small fingers remind me what I am missing. I hope to be more aware of my Father's steady grasp throughout my journey. What a blessing to walk with him. I am grateful he has given me granddaughters to remind me to hold on tight, to give me a picture of the joy and pleasure that come as I live life with him right beside me.

| Rita J. Platt |

Action Step:

This week, try to make a practice of extending your hand to your heavenly Father in the mornings before you even climb out of bed. Ask him to keep you near, keep you in his grip, and help you know the pleasure of living in his presence throughout the day.

Wisdom: We All Need It

> **"When she speaks, her words are wise, and she gives instructions with kindness."**
>
> —Proverbs 31:26

As I read this verse I wonder if I've been wise and kind. I certainly hope so. Being a mom brings many ups and downs. I wish I could say my children always did the right things and that they learned from each other, but that would not be a true statement.

I've always prayed for my girls to understand a real relationship with God and to fall in love with the man God has selected for them. I knew that if they would just keep their eyes on God, he would direct them and help them make wise decisions in life to include their partner for life.

My youngest daughter ran around with many young men, and to this day several of them are still best "buddies." She really thought she was in love with one young man, and he broke her heart. Now we know he was not who God had selected for her. Several months passed and she seemed to be much better. She played college softball, and my husband noticed a group of young men in his left field "spot" watching the game. Later we found out that one of those young men was the man God had selected for our daughter.

Before she was able to graduate, we got the call that she was pregnant. Not what I expected out of my Christian daughter who has helped many children understand what it means to really follow God. Now what wise words were there to say? God was with me, and all I could think was, "Babies are always a blessing." That is probably the wisest thing I have ever said, and I know it was directly from God. The key is that once we say something wise, we must not mess it up by saying something unkind. Thank goodness God gave me the right words to follow—we had a beautiful wedding and now have a beautiful grandson. My daughter will have a little time to stay home before she can complete her student teaching, but she is a great mom and her husband is a great dad. I'm so glad that God gave me the words of wisdom and kindness at the right time.

| Eliese McAllister |

Action Step:

Tell your children you love them every day, and let them know you pray for them. If you don't have a daily routine to pray with your children, start one. They will learn the importance of prayer from you.

Tasty Kitty Treats

> **" 'For I know the plans I have for you,' says the Lord. 'They are plans for good and not for disaster, to give you a future and a hope.' "**
> —Jeremiah 29:11

Hearing coughing, I rushed to find 1-year-old Ophelia happily feeding herself an unscheduled snack: cat food out of the bowl her sister was preparing for the kitties. I grimaced while fishing the broken pieces out of her mouth. Yet I was also thankful, knowing that she will suffer no real harm due to her curiosity.

Later that evening, having prepared a magnificently tender 10-pound pork roast, finely chopped cabbage simmered in juice from the roast, and fragrant jasmine rice steaming with garlic and real butter, I carefully mixed just the right proportions into a texture Ophelia could easily chew. After thanking God for our food, we ate ravenously…except for Ophelia. She very happily ate several bites, but then decided she had no interest in the beautiful culinary delight I had so meticulously planned and prepared. Instead, she munched on a few oyster crackers and was coaxed into swallowing a few bites of yogurt. Finally, after accepting that my plans for her dinner weren't working out, I released Ophelia from the high chair and set her on the floor to play.

ZOOM! Ophelia ran straight for the cat food bucket and snatched the bag of kitty treats to attempt another unscheduled snack.

Most children do grow out of putting gross items into their mouths. Unfortunately, they don't just grow up and decide every bit of "culinary perfection" placed before them is exactly what they wanted for breakfast/lunch/dinner. Additionally, older children who fully understand the love, planning, and preparation we put into their meal still sometimes reject or undervalue it. This is can be frustrating and difficult to understand.

How much more difficult is it for our God? He has prepared the perfect plan for our lives. He has taken the time to make it simple for us to understand by putting his commandments in writing for us to easily read, comprehend, and obey. Yet so often we gladly take a few bites of the perfect plan he has placed before us, just to turn right back to our own ways.

God's plan for a mother's life is far more fulfilling than any gourmet meal. Following our own plans is really far worse for us than crunching on a handful of dry cat food. Yet we all have an area of God's plan for our lives where we are tempted to crunch on cat food instead of feasting on the gourmet meal God planned for us.

| Lori Schmidtke |

Action Step:

What part of God's plan for your life do you have the hardest time giving up your plans for? Don't eat cat food today. Commit yourself to living off the feast God has so carefully planned for you. You will delight in the newfound ultimate satisfaction that only fully embracing God's plan can provide.

New Names, New Family

> "See how very much our Father loves us, for he calls us his children, and that is what we are! But the people who belong to this world don't recognize that we are God's children because they don't know him."
>
> —1 John 3:1

When my husband and I brought our son home from China, he was just over 2 years old. He had only known the name given to him by his orphanage. Although we worked diligently to keep part of his Chinese name, his identity was changing dramatically, and his new name reflected such.

He slowly came to understand that he belonged to a mom and dad who lovingly gave him a new name, and he embraced it. We had unintentionally not discussed that he had a new last name—a family identifier—until an unexpected, divine moment. One day I was picking up a prescription for him, and he heard me voice his full name. He repeated it softly, but it rang loudly in my heart. I turned to him and said, "That's right! Your last name is Riddle, just like Mama and Daddy's." He was overjoyed to share a last name with his mom and dad. I smiled through watery eyes as the truth of his adoption once again filled my soul: His new name came with a family.

I was also overwhelmed at the great truth of my own adoption into God's family. Through no merit of my own, God called me to himself and provided everything necessary to make me his own child. One day I will be given a new name, God's name, because he has made me his own (Revelation 3:12, 22:4).

Sometimes motherhood can be draining and discouraging. But sometimes God gives me a glimpse of his beauty, grace, and salvation through the life of my son. I can crawl into a great big blue funk with the mundane life of laundry, dishes, meals, and naps that occupy my daily life. But then I run to the pharmacy, and God showers me with such beauty that my heart might explode. I praise God for such grace and encouragement to remind me that he cares for me as his child and holds me in his righteous right hand at all times (Isaiah 41:10). My new identity as God's child gives purpose and beauty even in the mundane—not because they are always full of excitement but because my Father is present and is whispering beauty in all things, weaving my life into a picture that reflects his glory and beauty.

| Jenny Riddle |

Action Step:

As you go about your day today, look for ways that God reveals himself and his love to you through even the most mundane of tasks. Note these on your phone or other device so you can go back and visit these glimpses whenever you need encouragement.

Mom to Mom 10

Get together with one or two moms you know. Take time to talk about which of the devotions you've read recently was most meaningful to you and why. It's okay if you're all at different places in the book—just share what God puts on your heart.

Also, share an area of your life where you could use some prayer. Jot down what others say so you can remember to pray for them this week.

_____

_____

_____

_____

_____

When was the last time you got to see a movie that didn't have animated characters or superheroes? See if you and another mom or two can get together for a movie that you want to see—not one that your kids picked.

Mom Time!

Here's something fun to do with your family.

Read Aloud

Most moms read aloud to their children when the kids are young. But people of all ages love listening to a good story. Depending upon the ages of your children, choose a book that will take you a while to read, and take turns reading a chapter or two aloud each day. You might read a chapter aloud after breakfast—or your oldest child might read out loud to everyone else on the drive to school. For ideas on awesome books, check out scholastic.com/100books.

Living Between Chapters

> **"For I am about to do something new. See, I have already begun! Do you not see it?"**
> —Isaiah 43:19

Not long ago, I found myself a little lost. It felt as if life had paused in the middle of my story. Like I was living between chapters.

I lived in my sweet little home of almost 13 years. I loved it there. We raised our children in that home, had family get-togethers, fought, laughed, cried, killed bugs—you know, normal family stuff. Until our final child moved out.

Now that we had an empty nest, my husband and I decided to sell the house. Unfortunately, things didn't go as smoothly as planned, and before we knew it, we were dealing with escrow problems, loan issues, and not having a house to move into after ours had sold.

It was during those weeks, when we had no home to call our own, no more kids with us, and no clear future that I felt stuck, like I was living between chapters, having just ended the old one without starting a new. I felt busy but unproductive. I was existing but without a purpose.

With my house gone and mothering days nothing more than a memory, I began to feel the weight of all of the other areas of my life where I'd been living in between chapters—places where private dreams and great ambitions had been put on hold in order to focus my efforts on being a mom. I had been writing the chapter on motherhood for so long that I'd forgotten how to start a new one. I began anxiously waiting for a new chapter to start. I waited. And waited. And waited.

Thankfully, it wasn't too long before I had an epiphany: *If I want to begin a new chapter in my life, I can simply begin writing it.*

So I did. I began to ask God to show me what the content of that chapter might hold. For me, it turned out to be working on my book again. I pulled out the old manuscript and got down to business. I then shared my new venture with trusted friends who held me accountable, and before long, I was well into penning the next script of my life. And I have been writing ever since.

As I continue to write more and more chapters, I am reminded of how good God is to carry us through the in-between times, and how faithful he is to help coauthor the new.

| Sherri Stone-Bennett |

Action Step:

Perhaps, like me, you have dreams that have been put on hold. Take some time to create a bookmark: On one side, list one or two dreams you'd like to see unfold in the next chapter of your life. On the back, list a couple of Scriptures that will encourage you as you begin thinking about "writing" this new chapter.

"Jesus always used stories and illustrations like these when speaking to the crowds. In fact, he never spoke to them without using such parables."

—Matthew 13:34

When I first became a mother, I recognized my responsibility for the spiritual formation of my children. I remember feeling pressure to "do it right" so they would "get it." I wondered, "Do I need to learn to play the guitar so we could have a time of worship?" and "Do I need to go to seminary in order to offer a three-point theological sermon to my children?"

Then I remembered how my mother taught me something when I was a teenager. This everyday lesson profoundly affected my life. I remember it like it was yesterday. We were in the kitchen and she was about to make meringue for a pie. She put the egg whites in a bowl and told me to look in the bowl and tell her what I saw. I told her I saw through the egg whites to the bottom of the bowl.

Then she began to beat the egg whites until they became frothy. She again asked me what I saw, and I told her that I couldn't see to the bottom anymore.

She took the opportunity to explain to me that high school drama and conflict were much like the meringue. When a situation first arises, you can usually see what the problem is and seek to fix it. But if you keep beating the situation with gossiping, arguing, and taking sides, you will soon find yourself in a mess with your friends, unable to see through the drama anymore nor fix the situation.

This was parabolic teaching like Jesus'. He took the natural and used it to explain the spiritual. At that moment, all the pressure was off me to have a daily worship service with my children and simply live Jesus in front of them. As a mom, I've learned that the best way to lead my children spiritually is to use everyday moments as teachable ones. When I bathed my children, I would talk to them about how Jesus washes us clean. When I made them a peanut butter and jelly sandwich, I would tell them that Jesus is the friend that sticks closer than a brother. When I brushed their hair, I would tell them that God cares so much for them that every hair on their head was numbered. I simply began to look at life through "God-lenses" and shared his revelation to my children, in the everyday moments he supplied.

| Jena Forehand |

Action Step:

As you go throughout your day today, ask God to show you himself in the everyday things you do with your children. Share what he reveals to you with them. Take the pressure off yourself. Let God reveal, and you simply relay.

> **"Just as you cannot understand the path of the wind or the mystery of a tiny baby growing in its mother's womb, so you cannot understand the activity of God, who does all things."**
> —Ecclesiastes 11:5

When I was 36 weeks pregnant with my fourth child, I was told that our baby girl would be born with bone dysplasia, more commonly known as dwarfism. The joy inside me turned to grief and sorrow. Not because I didn't love this baby girl, but because I knew she would be different.

I reached out to everyone in prayer. Our church, our family, and our friends flooded me with verses and prayers, and I felt their comfort as I endured the emotional highs and lows. There were so many questions to be answered. I spent hours on the Internet researching, crying, and trying to understand why God thought this was something I could handle. How could I possibly do this? I wondered how we would explain this to our other children and family.

One day after visiting with doctors and nurses, I went home, crawled into bed, and sobbed. There was this fear inside me that I just couldn't shake. I read the verses and notes from my family over and over again, and nothing helped. I got out of bed and kneeled and prayed before God, "I love you and need you to comfort and hold me. Lord, please be near to me at this time."

I crawled back into bed and opened my Bible next to me and read a verse my sister had sent to me that week, "As thou knowest not what is the way of the spirit, nor how the *bones* do grow in the womb of her that is with child: even so thou knowest not the works of God who maketh all" (Ecclesiastes 11:5, King James Version, emphasis added). I stopped crying immediately and praised my God. God had a plan for my little girl. He created her bones. Who am I to question God's plan?

Four weeks later I held in my arms the most beautiful baby I had ever dreamed of. She has brought more joy than I could ever have imagined.

| Kristine Stark |

Action Step:

When waves of fear crash over you, reach for God's Word and search for his promises. Psalm 27:1 reminds us, "The Lord is my light and my salvation—so why should I be afraid? The Lord is my fortress, protecting me from danger, so why should I tremble?"

Just Get Away (or Just Go Away)

"Then Jesus went into a house to get away from the crowd."

—Mark 7:17

"Jesus went away and was hidden from them."

—John 12:36

"Then Jesus left them again and prayed the same prayer as before."

—Mark 14:39

Have you noticed that Jesus spent much of his ministry by himself? Of course, he led and counseled the disciples, he performed miracles, and he spoke to crowds. He also needed time to just get away, which, I have to admit, makes me feel so much better. There were times he went away to pray, and times he was just done. Other times we're not told what he did. I find myself guessing. Did he let off steam by working with his hands? Did he have a hobby? Did he go for a walk? Did he have the coveted-by-all-moms-everywhere treat of an afternoon nap?

Find time to just get away…in a good way.

Schedule a retreat day. Yes, with just a bit of planning, this can really happen. Take a day off work, or ask a friend to watch your children for the day. (You can return the favor later.) The point is to get out of your normal routine and spend some time—just you and God (and a good cup of coffee). Talk to him. Listen to him. Enjoy being with him.

Go for a walk. Now, there are times a good walk at the mall is in order, but I'm talking more about getting away into nature. If you don't live near nature, take a different route than you normally do. What do you see? What do you hear? What are you enjoying at this moment?

If you can't make a full day work, at least take a two-minute time-out. In the middle of a stressful day, lock yourself in the bathroom (I prefer the pantry—it has snacks). Think of something for which you're thankful—really thankful—and breathe. Then put the cheese puffs away, wipe your hands on your jeans, and rejoin the family.

Jesus didn't model an exact time table. It doesn't matter how long (or short) your time away may be. Just get away.

| Janna Firestone |

Action Step:

Depending on your schedule today, you might just have time for the two-minute time-out. But find the time to just go away. Breathe and be refreshed. Get away from the crowd. Pray. And block out a day, not too far down the road, for that retreat day.

Get together with one or two moms you know. Take time to talk about which of the devotions you've read recently was most meaningful to you and why. It's okay if you're all at different places in the book—just share what God puts on your heart.

Also, share an area of your life where you could use some prayer. Jot down what others say so you can remember to pray for them this week.

_____

_____

_____

_____

_____

Gather around a tablet, laptop, or other device and look at each other's pins on Pinterest—or peruse other social media sites you enjoy. Find a recipe to try, and laugh at the ones you'll never even know where to find the supplies for.

Mom Time!

Here's something fun to do with your family.

Record It

It's certain that someone in your family has a video camera—even if it's just on a phone. Make a commercial for your family, sharing why you're all so lucky to be related. Or record each other telling jokes, creating a cooking show, playing a musical instrument, doing cartwheels, or doing anything else that makes you smile.

Stillness in the Shadow

> **"He will cover you with his feathers. He will shelter you with his wings. His faithful promises are your armor and protection."**
>
> —Psalm 91:4

"Yes? What does that mean?" I asked my husband. I was too busy running around looking for the box to explain how to read the test, and I had missed the news!

Three weeks into our marriage, and we were a growing family.

Fast forward three years, and growing our family has not been nearly as easy as the early weeks of marriage.

With a miscarriage, a few months of hormone treatments, and two years of LH and HCG tests in the trash, I am left with a vast array of emotions and questions. If I try to make sense of it all, I only end up breathing into a brown paper bag. If I try to tell myself the cliché "Well, it's just God's plans, don't question," I'm left angry at a God who withholds good (who is not my God at all!).

In these moments, days, and years when the navigation and next steps of the journey are confusing, heartbreaking, and cloudy, I'm reminded to take a seat in the shadows.

When all feels hopeless.

When the storms of emotion blow in and around me.

When I find my head buried in my knees, my chest propelled up and down from the sobs—the aching too deep, too strong.

I take a seat in the dark. I hide in the shadows.

It can seem scary and lonely until I realize it's only because I'm in the safe shelter of God's wings, that his canopy covers me. There is warmth, comfort, and a pulsing heart I can feel beside me that I find I'm leaning into. I am far from being alone. I have nothing to fear because God will shelter me and hold me—for as long as I need.

| Kaylee Page |

Action Steps:

Find a timer (a little egg-shaped one, your phone, your microwave—anything that keeps time will work!). Find a dark room. Set your timer for 15 minutes. Sit. Breathe in and out. With each breath, picture yourself in the everlasting shelter provided. Feel the warmth of God's love touch your skin. Feel the beat of his heart pulse in you. Sit in the shelter for the entirety of those 15 minutes—and longer if you need to.

> **"Trust in the Lord with all your heart; do not depend on your own understanding. Seek his will in all you do, and he will show you which path to take."**
>
> —Proverbs 3:5-6

My son brings so much joy to my heart. His smile literally lights up any room that he enters. I am a very busy, single mom. I work two jobs, go to school full time, yet still have my ultimate, most rewarding job of being a mom. As an educator, I am very passionate about learning and try to encourage everyone around me to never stop learning, especially my son.

My son loves to learn, especially anything about animals. He has a learning disability and reading does not come very easy for him. After a long day of teaching, and then tutoring, it was time for me to do homework with my son. We were doing his reading homework and he was really struggling. He wanted to stop, but I kept pushing him to keep going. He was trying so hard, but the words just were not coming together. His eyes began to water. I asked him what was wrong and he replied, "Mommy, why is it that I try so hard but I can't read? I just want to be able to read like my friends." I began to cry with him and held him tightly. I told him that not only would he be able to read, but everything would click and he would be the best reader ever. I said, "When something is hard for Mommy, I take a deep breath and pray, but I never give up."

The next day we were about to start reading homework and my son said, "Wait, Mom, let's take a breath and pray before we read." My heart was overflowing. He still struggled while he was reading, but he did it with a smile and he seemed more encouraged than ever to do the best he could. I thought to myself: I am so blessed to be this little boy's mother.

| Stephanie Newson |

Action Step:

When times get tough, stop, take a deep breath, and lean on the Lord. He is always listening and provides comfort to you in your time of need.

An Aha Moment

> **"We can make our plans, but the Lord determines our steps."**
>
> —Proverbs 16:9

As a parent, I think it is a natural want to do what is best for our children. And so, like any good parent, the moment I realized I was having my first child, I was quick to begin my plans for her life. I wanted to teach her "this," and take her "here," and watch her do "that." Six months into her life, I discovered a surprise that caused me to rethink the direction her life would go. I found out I was pregnant.

I cried. I did not hold the instant excitement I had held with my former. Not because I was disappointed at having another child; I wanted more kids... eventually. I cried for my daughter because I feared how her life would change now that another would be entering it so soon. My attention would now be shared rather than focused on her many firsts. I knew I would tire easily during the pregnancy, therefore limiting my play. I feared for all the things she might now miss out on.

Needless to say, I had to quickly bounce out of this initial reaction; after all, another child of mine was on the way and he deserved as much love. I found myself pushing myself through the pregnancy, since I wanted to give my daughter everything she should have before the time to share her mom would come. Once my son arrived, I began to make efforts of exaggerated equal opportunities, still babying my baby as well as my baby girl.

As time has worn on with two infants in my home, I began to recognize the distinct differences in each child's personality. And over time, I noticed a dramatic shift in my attention. Where I once worried about what my daughter would miss out on, I did not comprehend what she might gain. My son and daughter are best friends now that they are older and, looking back, I recognize that the closeness in their age is part of the bond between the two. I realize that in the beginning this was not my plan, but looking back now, I would plan it no other way!

| Shelley Lake |

Action Step:

Think of a time something didn't go as you had planned. Now ponder the blessings you might have missed out on if it had. Take a moment to thank God for guiding your life in the direction according to his will, praying specific thanks for the blessings he has poured into your life.

> **"God decided in advance to adopt us into his own family by bringing us to himself through Jesus Christ. This is what he wanted to do, and it gave him great pleasure."**
>
> —Ephesians 1:5

At 9 years of age, I found myself the daughter of a single man who was looking for a wife and new mom for his three grade-school-aged girls. My mother had lost a difficult battle with cancer and now was with Jesus. After a deep time of mourning, my dad remembered that my mom had encouraged him to find someone whom he could love and who would also love and nurture us. So the journey began. I remember a date at the drive-in with all of us in tow and my sister locking the keys in the trunk. That was the last date with that woman!

My grandparents recommended that my dad ask out a beautiful young widow with flaming red hair. She loved God and was holding out for someone who would lead her in her faith and would also love and mentor her 2-year old son. After a very short courtship, my dad asked her to marry him and she accepted. They both took seriously the fact that they were accepting the other's children as well, and soon after, my new mom adopted my sisters and me while my dad adopted my new little brother. Even so, I was given the choice of what to call her and, for several months, I resolutely called her by name. I very vividly remember the first time I called her "Mom." It felt strange and yet relieved my young heart and made me feel like I belonged. I can see her lips curl to a smile in my memory of that moment. She had chosen me, and now I accepted and had chosen her as well.

When reading Ephesians 1, I feel an even deeper joy in the deliberate relationship that we can experience in God:

> *All praise to God, the Father of our Lord Jesus Christ, who has blessed us with every spiritual blessing in the heavenly realms because we are united with Christ. Even before he made the world, God loved us and chose us in Christ to be holy and without fault in his eyes. God decided in advance to adopt us into his own family by bringing us to himself through Jesus Christ. This is what he wanted to do, and it gave him great pleasure.*

Before my lifetime, God chose me…and he chose *you* as well. Many years ago, I accepted his gift and chose him to be my Father and share that relationship. Through the years, people would remark how much I looked like my "mom." She and I would exchange an "inside secret" glance and smile. What a fun bonus! In a similar and profound way, when we are a part of God's family we look like our holy, blameless heavenly Father.

| Lisa R. Young |

Action Steps:

Remind someone in your life that you choose to love them and to be in relationship. Say out loud that you are chosen by God and he loves you.

Get together with one or two moms you know. Take time to talk about which of the devotions you've read recently was most meaningful to you and why. It's okay if you're all at different places in the book—just share what God puts on your heart.

Also, share an area of your life where you could use some prayer. Jot down what others say so you can remember to pray for them this week.

_____

_____

_____

_____

_____

Give your mom friends flowers. Even if all you can afford are a couple of daisies or flowers picked from your yard, give them a fragrant and beautiful reminder that you love them—and that God does too!

Mom Time!

Here's something fun to do with your family.

Sweet Invention

Invite everyone into the kitchen to invent a new dessert.
Be willing to try anything, even if it sounds awful—some
families have discovered new favorites this way! One
teenaged guy wrapped a marshmallow in bacon and
roasted it over the grill for a new sweet and savory treat.
Another family wrapped candy and cookies in foil and
melted them all together to create "can-ookies" (candy
and cookies), which has now become a requested dessert.

Butting In

> **"And the Scriptures give us hope and encouragement as we wait patiently for God's promises to be fulfilled."**
>
> —Romans 15:4

A few years ago, our family was driving across town to go ice skating as snow fell heavily. Realizing the roads were worse than we had thought, my husband and I began to consider turning back and trying again on a clearer day. Just as protests from the kids began to erupt, we heard one of our daughters, who was 10 at the time, tell her twin sister in her most mature voice, "Let's be quiet until they make their decision; then we'll butt in."

I've felt the same many times. I know God is always faithful to fulfill his promises, but it seems that when life gets stormy, I despair. Just like my daughter, I start off with mature prayers and platitudes, but in a corner of my heart "butting in" is my backup plan. As the storm grows longer and I feel like God's promises aren't being fulfilled, I begin to butt in. I lie awake at night and tell him in great detail exactly how I think things should go moving forward. I beg and plead and cajole. I worry about what will happen if things don't go my way.

The great thing about God, though, is that the fulfillment of his promises doesn't hinge on my maturity, or lack thereof. I am precious and loved by him, regardless of whether I'm praying in my mature voice or I'm "butting in." He keeps me in his tender care. When the time is right, and despite the storms, his promises will faithfully be fulfilled. He will calm my heart and quiet my fears. I am in his hands—and so are you.

| Sarah Mendez |

Action Step:

Reflect for a few moments on God's truth about his promises. Grab a marker (dry erase works best, but permanent can be used too and later removed with rubbing alcohol). Go to a mirror you use frequently (the mirror on your car visor, your bedroom or bathroom mirror) and write a reminder to yourself about this truth. When you see your reflection in the mirror, remember you are precious to God and are in his tender care—and he is faithful to keep his promises.

> "He gives power to the weak and strength to the powerless. Even youths will become weak and tired, and young men will fall in exhaustion. But those who trust in the Lord will find new strength. They will soar high on wings like eagles. They will run and not grow weary. They will walk and not faint."
>
> —Isaiah 40:29-31

I've always loved this passage. Long before I was a mom, I'd underlined these verses in my Bible, and written them on a notecard to stick to my fridge. I remember catching this verse out of the corner of my eye one day while making laps around the kitchen carrying my teething twin boys. The phrase that stuck out was, "young men will fall in exhaustion." I laughed out loud, probably a bit hysterically, thinking that at some point these cranky, tired boys would eventually grow tired and sleep. Then I could lay my weary head down somewhere for a few moments of rest.

As moms, we're weary all the time. When I was pregnant with my first child, everyone warned me about the sleepless first nights. No one told me I would never feel truly rested again. Long after the newborn phase, moms are up at night soothing nightmares, helping children go potty, waiting anxiously for children to come home, or worrying and praying for grown children already out of the house.

In our own strength, we can't be the moms we want to be. We're worn out and tired, but God extends his strength to us and gives us power when we're weak. When we trust in the Lord, he will renew our strength.

| Amy Weaver |

Action Step:

To put our trust in the Lord, we need to shift our focus from the wearying details of the day back to God. Find a verse you can draw strength from. Maybe it's an old standby or one you specifically look up based on where you're struggling right now. Write out the verse and place it somewhere you'll see it often. Allow God's Word to give you strength and power when you're weak and tired.

Sweethearts and Teapots

> **"A gentle answer deflects anger, but harsh words make tempers flare."**
>
> —Proverbs 15:1

*N*ow sweetheart, don't hit your brother. I heard moms at preschool gymnastics talk so calmly and gently when their children acted up, it made me want to scream. Why couldn't I keep calm and carry on in such a sweet tone?

After several weeks of observing the few moms who had mastered this technique, I discovered the secret. They always talked in a higher pitch when correcting their children. Yep, that was it. So I tried it. It worked! Honest, it did.

Not only did it keep me from exploding, it made my kids settle down. I think it was because they thought I had totally lost my mind, but the important thing was that it worked. At first they responded out of curiosity and amazement. Then they responded because they couldn't stand to hear me talk like that.

They're teenagers now and the gentle technique has changed a bit. The high pitch is in my head but it isn't gentle. It's more like the sound of a teapot with steam pouring out of my eyes, ears, and nose. The trick now is to keep my mouth closed until the water cools. If I wait, I'm better able to keep from burning my kids or myself with the words that I spout. That's not easy considering their age, and I don't always keep my mouth shut when I should.

What's worse is that I recognize my words do more than cause a momentary flare of tempers. I feel it inside me and see it in my kids. One child burns with guilt when harsh words are splashed on him. Another child's temperament creates a shield that exports her to another world or deflects the anger back on me. Either way, either personality, harsh words singe a relationship.

As moms, we would like to always do the right thing and never have to apologize. Wouldn't that be great? However, I'm learning that an apology is often the best teacher. It allows us to point out the truth of God's Word and our own need to grow in its personal application. Harsh words make tempers flare whether they are in the home or elsewhere. Gentle words can cool the steaming water of any teapot. Teaching our kids how to cool tempers, theirs or others', is a valuable lesson.

| Lisa Biggs Crum |

Action Step:

Keep some small candy nearby. When your little (or grown) sweetheart causes your teapot to steam, occupy your mouth for a bit with a piece of candy, and then give a gentle answer from the sweetness of Jesus in your heart. If the harsh words flow from your mouth, apply the soothing ointment of "I'm sorry" and try not to use the word "but" in your apology. If you use a computer regularly, add Proverbs 15:1 to your screensaver or desktop background.

Perfect Offerings

> "And you are living stones that God is building into his spiritual temple. What's more, you are his holy priests. Through the mediation of Jesus Christ, you offer spiritual sacrifices that please God."
>
> —1 Peter 2:5

My 6-year-old daughter Jessica loves to give me gifts. Whenever we're out somewhere and she spies a particularly lovely flower, acorn, or leaf, she picks it up and presents it to me. When we're at home, she draws pictures of the two of us with hearts floating all around our heads to show how much we love each other.

I always make sure to tell Jessica how much I appreciate each thing she gives me, and then I get to watch her little face light up with satisfaction.

Are her gifts perfect? No. Very rarely is an object from nature without blemish, and her drawings are the drawings of a 6-year-old. But even though they are not technically perfect, they are flawless in one important way: They perfectly demonstrate her heart toward me.

That's why I love what she gives me—because when I receive a gift from her, I receive not only some special object, but also a very real demonstration of her love. And that warms my mother-heart.

It's a Good Thing Children Are a Treasure...They've Broken All My Other Ones

In the same way, God loves to receive gifts from you and me—gifts not only of our money, but of our time, our expressions of love, and our praise. Our prayers may not be the most eloquent thoughts he's ever heard, but that doesn't matter. Neither is there any such thing as our sincere service and time-offerings not being up to his standards. God loves receiving anything we give him when we give with a right heart.

I don't want Jessica to wait until she can draw perfectly or until she finds the perfect flower before giving it to me. Likewise, God doesn't want us to wait until we can design something elaborate for him. He is pleased with anything we offer that comes from love.

| Megan Breedlove |

Action Step:

Go to God in prayer. Offer him the best praise you have—and know that he receives it gladly and that his heart is moved. Ask him if there are any other gifts he would like to receive from you.

Get together with one or two moms you know. Take time to talk about which of the devotions you've read recently was most meaningful to you and why. It's okay if you're all at different places in the book—just share what God puts on your heart.

Also, share an area of your life where you could use some prayer. Jot down what others say so you can remember to pray for them this week.

_____

_____

_____

_____

_____

_____

Celebrate your friendship with other moms by going out for something sweet. Cupcakes? Pie? A sweet cup of hot cocoa? Laugh together, cry together, share life together. Friendship is sweet.

Mom Time!

Here's something fun to do with your family.

Journal of Random Thoughts

This is a fun project to start in the summer when school is out—but it works no matter what time of year. Give each of your children an inexpensive journal or notebook. Write a note to your child and date it. Then explain that this is a way to write notes back and forth to each other. You can write a note and tell your child stories about your day or your childhood or anything else. You can also ask them questions. Then you'll leave the journal where they can find it and write notes and stories and questions back to you.

This is especially nice for children who are not very "chatty." They may feel more comfortable opening up in a different way than through conversation. You can also try having just one journal for the entire family to write in and leave notes to each other—with the guidelines that all notes need to be positive and encouraging. ☺

Notes

Notes

144